"It has never been more important to have your own personal brand and to promote what makes you unique—and this goes for executives, small-business owners, and everyone in between. In *Be Your Own Best Publicist*, experts Jessica and Meryl have illustrated how to cleverly use PR to build your own brand with some great ideas—not to mention some entertaining stories."

—Martin Lindstrom, brand advisor and *New York Times* best-selling author of *Buyology: The Truth and Lies About Why We Buy*

"No matter what your career or business goals, *Be Your Own Best Publicist* will provide you with invaluable advice on how to present yourself more effectively, communicate more clearly, and succeed more quickly. Jessica and Meryl share their own insider tips as well as anecdotes and insights from an impressive group of experts. It's like having your own personal PR team on call."

—Lindsey Pollak, author, *Getting from College to Career*

"Not all publicists are created equal, but Jessica and Meryl have managed to capture and gather the best advice from leaders in various industries, as well as their own powerful experiences, in this must-read bible which will undeniably connect you, your product, or your company to the next level."

—Heidi Krupp, CEO of K2, Krupp Kommunications

Be Your Own Best Publicist

Be Your Own Best Publicist

How to Use PR Techniques
to Get Noticed, Hired,
and Rewarded at Work

Jessica Kleiman
&
Meryl Weinsaft Cooper

CAREER
PRESS

Pompton Plains, N.J.

BE YOUR OWN BEST PUBLICIST
EDITED BY NICOLE DEFELICE
TYPESET BY KATHRYN HENCHES
Cover design by Rob Johnson
Printed in the U.S.A.

To order this title, please call toll-free 1-800-CAREER-1 (NJ and Canada: 201-848-0310) to order using VISA or MasterCard, or for fur-ther information on books from Career Press.

The Career Press, Inc.
220 West Parkway, Unit 12
Pompton Plains, NJ 07444
www.careerpress.com

Library of Congress Cataloging-in-Publication Data
Kleiman, Jessica.
  Be your own best publicist : how to use PR techniques to get
noticed, hired, and rewarded at work / by Jessica Kleiman and Meryl
Weinsaft Cooper.
    p. cm.
  Includes bibliographical references and index.
  ISBN 978-1-60163-148-0 -- ISBN 978-1-60163-724-6 (ebook)
    1. Public relations. 2. Career development. 3. Publicity.
  I. Cooper, Meryl Weinsaft. II. Title.

HD59.K58 2011
650.1-- dc22

                                                2010043708

Acknowledgments

Most public relations professionals strive to stay behind the scenes, orchestrating from a safe distance as their clients enjoy the spotlight. With this book, we're emerging from off-stage with the express purpose of helping others promote themselves and their talents, so they can be rewarded in their careers, just as we have been rewarded in ours.

We toyed with the idea of writing a career guide for a couple years, but it wasn't until our agent Ryan Fischer-Harbage said to us, "Think about what makes you uniquely qualified to write a book," that the proverbial light bulb went off, and we realized that we could use the skills and techniques we've honed throughout our collective 30-plus years in the PR industry and teach others how to apply them to their own careers.

If it weren't for the people who exist behind the scenes in our lives, we wouldn't have been able to finish this book. Jessica would like to thank her wonderful husband, Tommy, a fellow writer who pushes her to be her best every single day; their beautiful daughter, Emma, who was born the week the book was sold (and whose mommy wrote instead of napping during her maternity leave!); Rayna Gillman, the best mother, friend, and editor a girl could ask for; and the rest of her amazing family, who have always given her an abundance of love and support, both personally and professionally. Jessica is also grateful to have spent the past decade at Hearst Magazines, where she continues to be inspired and excited every day by the creative, talented people with whom she works, and who make her a better PR professional as a result. And, of course, Meryl, a fantastic partner and friend, whom she sometimes felt operated as the other half of her brain during the writing and editing process.

Meryl thanks her incredible husband (and love of her life), Chris, who lent his keen storytelling talent and strong shoulder of support throughout the writing process and beyond. Her gratitude extends to her sisters, Pamela and Sima, both of whom continue to be great editors and even better friends. She also thanks her parents, Bernard Weinsaft, Ina Bari, and Larry Hornstein, all of whom consistently encourage her to pursue her passion and persevere. Of course, she is supremely grateful for the wonderful clients and cohorts with whom she's worked over the years—especially key members of the Vice Squad, past and present (you know who you are). Most importantly, she thanks her amazing coauthor Jessica, who moved heaven, earth, weekly meetings, and baby carriage to write this book, and made this process a true pleasure.

A special thank-you to Nora O'Malley, our research assistant, who did a yeoman's job of wrangling experts and reading our draft chapters. To Simon Alexander and Sadah Saltzman, whose hair, makeup, and photography skills helped us present our best image. And our undying appreciation goes to our talented editor, Nicole DeFelice, who whipped the book into shape, as well as the entire team at Career Press, who gave us lots of personal attention and the support to share this book with the world.

Finally, to our friends, colleagues, and mentors in public relations and beyond, whose invaluable wisdom and support helped make us the publicists we are and this book what it is, we thank you from the bottom of our hearts. A special nod goes to the following people for taking the time to share their anecdotes and advice: Kristen Angus, Phillip Bloch, Stacey Blume, Anna Brand, Alec Brownstein, Erin Busbee, Amanda Casgar, Sarah Clagett, Beth Thomas Cohen, Scott Cooke, Linda Descano, Alison Schwartz Dorfman, Janine Driver, Steve Dumain, Steve Farnsworth, Maggie Gallant, Nina Garcia, Adam Glassman, Davidson Goldin, Tom Handley, Jane Hanson, Matthew Hiltzik, Melissa Hobley, Carrie Horn, Leigh Hurst, Christine Kaculis, Micah Jesse Koffler, Heidi Krupp, Michael Lazerow, Sheryl Victor Levy, Shaun Lee Lewis, Jonny Lichtenstein, Mary Mayotte, Bill McGowan, Dana Fields Muldrow, Sheila Munguia, Joyce Newman, Joshua Persky, Shant Petrosssian, Lindsey Pollak, Susan Portnoy, Karen Robinovitz, Shawn Sachs, Alexander Samuelson, Matt Schwartz, Peter Shankman, Lisa Sharkey, Sarah Shirley, Dayna Spitz, Ronn Torossian, Laurel Touby, Michael Volpatt, Jayne Wallace, Patti Wood, Alicia Ybarbo, and Jennifer Zweben.

Contents

Introduction

"Without promotion something terrible happens.... Nothing!
—P.T. Barnum

Shakespeare astutely observed, "All the world's a stage, and all the men and women merely players." What he failed to mention is that not all the roles available are created equal. While some get to be Hamlet, others are relegated to standing in the background. Ending up center stage requires a perfect storm of talent, timing, planning, and (oh yeah) luck. That's where public relations comes in: Part art, part science, PR can help propel you into the spotlight, whether you're looking for a job, hoping to build a business, or trying to get that once-in-a-lifetime professional role.

From Phineas Taylor (P.T.) Barnum, creator of the Barnum & Bailey Circus (who has been called the father of publicity), to the carefully crafted images of celebrities such as Lady Gaga and George Clooney, publicity has played an important role in the careers of some of the most famous—and infamous—people. But it isn't only celebrities who can use public relations and the art of self-promotion to attract attention; anyone can—including you. Most everyday people can't afford to hire their own publicist to help them build a personal platform or image that makes an impact, so the goal of this book is to teach you how to apply, to your own career, the practices and skills PR professionals have used during the past century to influence public opinion. We're here to help you craft the language that represents "brand you," and give you the tools to communicate that consistently, clearly, and succinctly.

Are you reentering the workforce or changing careers altogether? Looking for a new or first job? Trying to lock in that promotion or land that new client? Whatever your milestone moment, you can learn to use the same classic techniques that we've employed throughout our collective 30-plus years in PR to help clients (from media companies, and luxury brands, restaurants, and hotels, to high-profile personalities) build their reputations, gain attention, and stand out from the competition. In today's world, where image is paramount and your digital footprint is set in cement, it is even more crucial to be your own best publicist, advocate, and cheerleader in the workplace.

So what is PR, really? According to the Chartered Institute of Public Relations, the largest public relations organization in Europe, "PR is about reputation—the result of what you do, what you say and what others say about you…the discipline which looks after reputation, with the aim of earning understanding and support and influencing opinion and behavior. It is the planned and sustained effort to establish and maintain goodwill and mutual understanding between an organization and its publics."

In short, PR is designed to build and protect one's reputation and image. Creating and maintaining a reputation is just as important for individuals as it is for organizations.

In the following pages, we offer tools, techniques, and tactics that will help you take center stage in your life and make a positive splash in the workplace, breaking the process into three distinct parts, called The Three Ps: Prepare, Project and Protect. When learning how to be your own best publicist, you first need to *prepare* by developing your personal story, doing research, and mapping out a plan to reach your goals. Then, you need to *project* your personality, image, and key messages. Lastly, once you've accomplished the first two steps, you want to make sure to *protect* the image you've created.

In addition to personal anecdotes and firsthand accounts drawn from both our experiences and those of our key industry contacts, we'll share tips about networking, how to ace interviews, build message points, garner respect at work, and other important tactics that will help anyone succeed in his or her career, called out in the following ways:

- **Fact Check:** Stats and figures to illustrate the chapter topic.
- **Key Message:** Advice or tidbits of information from an industry pro who has "been there, done that."
- **News Flash:** Anecdotes/news from the trenches that also share important takeaways.
- **One-on-One Interviews:** Q&A with a key expert.
- **Sound Bite:** Quotes that drive the message home.

At the end of every chapter, you'll be invited to create your own deliverables for a personal PR action plan by discerning what makes you unique, writing sample pitch letters, or trying out networking techniques, for example.

Key Messages:
Top 10 guiding PR principles

We polled our friends and colleagues in the PR industry to come up with the tenets that drive our business, all of which can translate to yours, whatever it may be. Each of the following will be addressed in the book:

1. **Communicate clearly.** Know how to get your message across loud and clear, whether in writing or verbally.
2. **Be fearless.** If you never ask, you will never know.
3. **Be proactive and responsive.** Anticipate challenges or obstacles and, if they arise, address them quickly.
4. **Play nicely in the sandbox with others.** PR, like other industries, is about collaboration. Be kind, receptive, and respectful to those around you, and maintain a positive attitude.
5. **See stories everywhere.** Pay attention to what's going on around you and let it inspire and inform you.
6. **Be the expert.** Do your homework, but also trust your instincts. You know your strengths and talents better than anyone else does.
7. **Be "streative."** Strike a balance between creativity and strategy.
8. **Fail forward.** Learn from your mistakes, and don't beat yourself up when you make them.
9. **Be passionate.** Love and believe in what you do.
10. **Be resourceful and flexible.** Leave no stone unturned, and be open to new developments and ways of doing things.

Whether your goal is to land a new job, gain recognition in your current one, start a business, or grow the one you already have, leveraging the core principles of PR can help you establish your own personal brand, expand your network of connections, and position yourself as an expert and a valuable resource, ultimately allowing you to move up the ladder of success.

PREPARE

*"Winning can be defined
as the science of being
totally prepared."*
—George Allen

Chapter 1

Communication Is Key

"Effective communication is 20 percent what you know and 80 percent how you feel about what you know."
—Jim Rohn, American businessman

"So, tell me about yourself." You'd be surprised at how difficult it is for most people to explain their ideas or respond to that question in a quick and succinct fashion.

To be successful in PR, you must master how to communicate effectively—both in writing and while speaking—with clients, colleagues, coworkers, media, and the public. When we pitch the media, we only have about 30 seconds to impress them and capture their attention, or risk losing our opportunity to "sell" them on whatever angle we're presenting. This "30 Second Rule" applies whether we're pitching via phone, in person, or through e-mail. Reporters and producers are busy people who are regularly bombarded with hundreds of pitches from eager PR folks trying to get their client or story into the news or on TV. Similarly, human-resources folks receive innumerable resumes and cold calls from prospective job candidates every day, and potential clients may

not be so keen to take a call or entertain a meeting with someone they don't know.

In an age where people's attention spans are getting shorter
and shorter—partially because they are inundated by distrac-
tions such as e-mail, Twitter, and cell phones—30 seconds is
a veritable eternity. Knowing how to communicate concisely
and clearly will help you hook the interest of whomever you're
pitching, whether for a job, a promotion, a new assignment, or
prospective business.

Before you reach out to market yourself or your ideas in
the workplace, it's vital to spend some time thinking about
your elevator pitch, which, according to *Businessweek* (June
2007), is "the quick, succinct summation of what your company makes or does, so named because it should last no longer
than the average elevator ride." The most effective ones are
easy to understand and get to the point right away. After all,
theoretically, you only have about a half a minute. Here are
some tips for coming up with your own:

- **Know your goal.** If you are seeking a job or a promotion, your pitch should focus on what you could
  bring to the company or position. If you're selling
  your services as a freelancer or vendor, think about
  what makes you the right fit for your potential client or employer.

- **Have a good hook.** In PR, the unique hook or angle of your story is what attracts the interest of the
  media. What's *your* differentiating factor? What
  makes you an intriguing story? What about you
  would pique someone's interest? For example, one
  of Jessica's staffers used to be a television producer
  and, during her job interview, she made a point to
  mention her experience booking talent and working behind-the-scenes on a talk show. Because so

much of our business is figuring out what makes a great story or an appealing television segment, the fact that she worked on the "other side" and understood what producers look for made her an attractive hire. One other important note: Are you a rock climber or world traveler? Were you a mentor to a coworker? Do you have a strong following on Twitter? Make sure your resume highlights your hook. It offers the interviewer a way to connect, and could help you stand out from the competition.

Key Message:
Remember the five Cs of pitching

According to Tom Handley, professor at Parsons The New School for Design, there are five Cs to remember when you're pitching your product or yourself:

- **C**reative. Always have a unique hook.
- **C**oncise. Keep it tight and on point.
- **C**lear. Have a firm understanding of the key points or differentiating factors.
- **C**ontent. Include all pertinent information.
- **C**atcher. Know who you're pitching; know what the person has done, and his or her track record, so you can give your pitch in the right way to that person.

News Flash:
Don't be afraid to rehearse

Similar to actors running their lines, successful publicity opportunities are realized via significant preparation and practice. Former television producer Lisa Sharkey tells us, "When I was a producer at *Good Morning America*, I would give guests a little speech in the green room. A lot of people with amazing stories have never been on camera before, and it was intimidating for them to have to be on air with Diane Sawyer. It can be just as intimidating to meet or interview with a big executive or potential boss. So how do you handle that? I would say to them, 'Just speak from the heart.' Also, it was extremely important to rehearse as many times as needed until they got it right. I worked with a now regular contributor who had never been on TV before, and we'd sometimes rehearse 20 or 30 times."

Body language expert and professional speaker Patti Wood suggests practicing with props and positions that reflect the setting in which you'll be speaking: Will you be at a podium? What kind of chair will be provided? She explains, "Sitting on a stool requires a lot more coordination than sitting on a chair. It's good to know so you can plan ahead and visualize the interview from start to finish." Wood recalls a personal experience where she was interviewed for *Live with Regis and Kelly*; she found out the night before that, because the segment was about couples' body language when they go to sleep, the interview would be done reclining on a bed with Regis. That evening, she spent a few hours laying on the bed in her hotel room, rehearsing each question and answer to ensure she was prepared and relaxed for the next morning. She aced the interview.

The Takeaway: The best way to stave off nerves and ensure the best delivery is to practice your pitch in a setting and situation that mimics where you will be speaking. If you're presenting to a new client, practice in a boardroom or at a desk. If you're negotiating a promotion or raise, run through your arguments in the conference room or envision yourself in your boss's office. Interviewing for a new position? Rehearse the Q&A with a friend to make sure you're prepared.

 Sound Bite

"Once a word goes out of your mouth,
you can never swallow it again."
—A Russian proverb

Pull It Together

A classic PR tool—and one that we have both used to great success during our careers—is the press kit, a promotional packet of materials that includes all the background information about a company or product, including bios of key executives, fact sheets, testimonials and, in some cases, relevant photos or images. Often, the centerpiece of this kit is a press release, a written announcement of news about a person, product, event, or place that is typically sent to media to generate interest in the topic at hand, and provide them with all the pertinent details they need to cover it. Some of you reading this book might have occasion to draft your own press release— say, if you are announcing a new business venture or are pitching your services as a freelancer. But even if you never do, you can leverage some key elements and tactics used to create one to effectively share your own story:

- **Timing is everything.** In writing and servicing press releases, timing is of the utmost importance. Be sure you're offering the most up-to-date information in whatever you do.
- **Have an attention grabbing headline.** Consider it your opening line or greeting. What's going to make a memorable impression? This could apply to an e-mail between colleagues, a letter to a prospective employer, or a note to a potential client.
- **Don't bury the lead.** Shant Petrossian, producer of a top morning show implores, "Give 'em what they want on top...[and] support it with a great example." Fellow morning-show producer Sarah Clagett concurs. "Who has the time to listen to a five-minute voicemail or phone pitch before the key points are made? If you want to grab

my attention, bullet-point out the most important elements first. If I'm interested, I'll ask you to fill in the additional information afterwards."

Maggie Gallant, senior vice president at Rogers & Cowan, warns about "the hummingbird effect." She suggests thinking of people "as a hummingbird who will listen (or read) for a second and then move on." In other words, get the important messages out first, and in a way that people can receive them.

- **The devil's in the details.** When crafting your story, address the information needed to make the point, including the five Ws—Who? What? When? Where? Why?

- **Talk it out.** Once the release is written, read it aloud to ensure that it makes sense, is to the point, and sounds like something an actual human being would say. When we draft a quote on behalf of our clients or executives for a release or press statement, we want it to sound conversational, not stilted. We always ask ourselves: Is the language easy to understand? Does it include anything that someone outside your industry wouldn't know? Are the messages or quotes strong enough to stand behind when you see them covered in a media outlet?

Whether or not you decide you need a press release, you should still write a bio (you can craft it using your resume as a guide), a fact sheet outlining your talents and services (if appropriate), and have samples of your work, references, and/or testimonials at the ready. Matt Schwartz, founder of MJS Executive Search, says it's also important to prepare case studies to highlight your accomplishments. "By offering an overview of the situation, sharing any challenges you encountered, and including the results generated, you can give potential clients or employers a clear sense of who you are and what you would do if you worked with their company." Walking into an interview with your own personal press kit will help differentiate you from the rest of the candidates. If you have a Website, make it a one stop shop for information about you by posting all of your materials there, too.

What's With the Attitude? Everything.

Attitude is an extremely important factor in public relations, not to mention when you're up for a job opening, promotion, plum assignment, or new business. Showing poise, enthusiasm, and willingness to work hard often goes further than just being the most qualified person for the gig. There's nothing worse than a bad attitude from an employee, coworker, or vendor. It's like going to a great restaurant, but having an obnoxious waiter: the food and setting may be of high quality, but if the service stinks, you're unlikely to return or recommend it to others. Particularly in this day and age, when companies are paying closer attention to their bottom line and making fewer hires and promotions, having a positive outlook and a team- player mentality will win you extra points in the workplace.

Here is some advice that will help you steer clear of an attitude-generated misstep:

- **Never say "That's not my job."** With smaller staffs and more to do, companies are asking employees to take on bigger roles, sometimes with assignments that fall outside of their exact job description. If you want to move up and be valuable, take on the extra assignment, even if it's not in your wheelhouse. You may learn something new. The worst reaction when a boss or client asks you to go above and beyond the norm is to complain that it's not your job to do such-and-such. If you're a math-challenged writer and you're being asked to do the company's accounting, then it's okay to say, "I'm more than willing to take on extra work, but I'm afraid that accounting is not my strong suit, and I don't want to let you down. Is there another assignment you need help with that's more appropriate to my skill set?" That way, you're turning down the request because you lack the knowledge to handle it properly, not because it's technically not your job.

- **Watch your expressions.** We've all seen it: people rolling their eyes or making faces behind their boss' back when they hear something they don't like. Though you may think no one notices, it's just bad form. Keep your negative thoughts inside and, to take a cue from Lady Gaga, learn to have a poker face (or even better, a happy face!) in front of others.

- **Quit your complaining.** We all have moments at work where we're annoyed at our boss, colleague, or client, and are tempted to whine about the situation to coworkers or office friends. Here's the thing: complaining in the workplace is not only unprofessional, but it's also dangerous—not to mention negative PR for yourself. You may think you can trust that cubicle mate with whom you eat lunch every day, but she very well could be angling for an assignment or promotion that you're up for and now you've armed her with the knowledge that you're unhappy about something at work. If you're truly upset about a situation, set up a meeting with your boss, client, or colleague to address it in a professional, clear way instead of griping about it behind their backs. When you've had a bad day or someone has rubbed you the wrong way one time too many, save your rants for later when you can safely air your grievances to your best friend, mom, or spouse.

- **Don't stew in your own juices.** People aren't mindreaders, so just say what you mean. Instead of sighing and muttering to your boss, "I guess I'll just stay late again" because you have so much work to do, sit down with her and say, "I appreciate the additional responsibility you've given me, but I'm trying to figure out how to get everything done within normal working hours. Though I don't mind staying late on occasion, it would help me to hear from you what projects take priority so I can tackle those first." That way, you can get clear direction from your supervisor instead of toiling away every night until you get bitter or burned out. Had Jet Blue flight attendant Steven Slater, whose meltdown made headlines in August 2010, communicated his frustration about how customers were treating him instead of letting it boil over, he might have avoided his "I'm mad as hell, and I'm not gonna take it anymore" moment, saving his job and keeping him out of trouble.
- **Don't give up.** In PR, if we took no for an answer, we'd never get anything done. There have been plenty of times when we've pitched a story over and over again, only to be met with rejection. But on the 10th try, after researching a new reporter,

or trying a different angle, we got a bite. In her best-selling book *Basic Black: The Essential Guide to Getting Ahead at Work (and in Life)*, Hearst Magazines' former chairman Cathie Black tells of her frustration when she first arrived at the company and repeatedly heard the refrain "we tried that already" in response to ideas. That phrase screams of a defeatist attitude. Either try it again, or explore another avenue. Or, as Black suggests in her book, ask yourself, "Why didn't the idea work originally? What was the fallout, and what did we learn?" By remaining goal-oriented and opening yourself up to alternate routes to success, you'll be a lot more fruitful (more on that in Chapter 10).

Anything You Say Can and Will Be Held Against You

In public relations, we consider everything on the record, even if it's technically off the record (meaning a member of the media promises to keep the information you provide on background only and not for public attribution). However, to steal a phrase from one of our mentors, "We're paid to be paranoid." So we ascribe to the philosophy that you shouldn't say anything aloud or in writing that you don't want to see in print. Most people know you have to be careful about what you write, because it could end up reaching a lot more people than intended. With the proliferation of e-mail, texting, and Tweeting, it's simply too easy for a message to be forwarded, even if it was just meant for one person's eyes.

When it comes to interviews, less is definitely more. First, if one of our clients or executives rambles on during a media interview, that reporter has far more quotes to choose from— and often the one negative or critical thing said is what makes it into the story. When this happens, the person quoted is usually surprised and angry but, frankly, if he said it, there's not much we can do. Second, our TV producer friends tell us that they likely won't invite someone back if the host couldn't get in a word edgewise during the segment. The same principle applies whether you're in a pitch meeting or job interview: you want to answer the questions, but not make the session into a droning monologue. No one needs to hear about your sick cat or your job history dating back to when you worked in an ice cream parlor in high school. Stay focused on the interviewer's questions and stick to the facts that matter.

 Key Message:
They have you at "hello"

According to media trainer Patti Wood, "I tell my clients to read various celebrity interviews and see how many times the journalist will comment about the notable's house, yappy dog, or how he/she answers the phone. It's important to note that *everything* is on the record, and to be cognizant of what you say and do at all times when dealing with an interview."

The Takeaway: It's vital to be "on"—or at your best—from the moment you pick up the telephone or walk into the office building for an interview.

Hanging on the Telephone

In our business, it's imperative to "get on the horn." We're all guilty of relying too heavily on e-mail and text messaging, but there's something to be said for the good old-fashioned tactic of picking up the telephone. When you actually hear a person's voice, it creates an immediate personal connection. A phone conversation also enables you to have a real dialogue versus a choppy back-and-forth via e-mail or no response at all (which can happen if your message ends up in junk mail hell). More often than not, you'll get a quicker answer by phone. We'll typically call reporters to pitch a story so we can chit-chat a bit, ask them how their summer's been, or compliment them on a recent story before going in for the kill. Here are some other tricks of the PR trade when it comes to phone-call pitching and follow-up:

- **Take the temperature.** When calling a busy person, we always ask if it's a good time. He or she will tell you if it isn't and be more amenable to re-scheduling. What's more, your thoughtfulness will be appreciated.

- **Use your name and number as "bookends."** If you get someone's voice mail, clearly give your name and phone number first, and then repeat it again at the end. That way, if the recipient missed your name or number, they don't have to replay the entire message to get your contact info. Make it easy for people to get back to you, and you'll increase the odds that they will.

- **Never leave bad news on a voice mail.** While it's tempting to offload the negative news onto an impersonal voice mailbox, in PR you learn quickly that it's better to share that kind of information in person, or one-on-one via the phone. First, you can't prove that someone actually got the message if you didn't actually talk to him or her. Second, with sensitive information, it's always better to ensure that it lands the way you want it to. Third, if it's disappointing someone, you want to be able to speak directly with the person to smooth over any ruffled feathers.

- **Focus, people.** Ever get messages from people that ramble on as if you actually had answered the phone? Or, they're leaving you a message while yelling at their kids, paying for their cab ride, or ordering a cocktail? Take a page out of the public relations handbook and pay attention to what the other person is saying. The danger of being distracted may lead to missed opportunities to tell your story or to clear up a misconception.

- **Know what you want to say.** It sounds like a no-brainer, but when you finally get an important person on the phone, you need to be ready to launch into the conversation easily and quickly, instead of hemming and hawing until you can gather your thoughts. If it helps, write down bullet points or notes in advance so you can refer to them during your call.

Get It in Writing

In our world, there is another cardinal rule: get things in writing. It's extremely helpful to have a paper trail of exactly what was said or agreed upon with clients, colleagues, or the media. For example, we will often respond to a press inquiry with a written statement sent via e-mail, versus picking up the phone in case something is misinterpreted in a verbal conversation. Or, if we do have a phone chat or conference call, we'll follow it up with a recap note outlining what was discussed and the next steps. If you get a job offer, ask for an official offer letter before committing. If you have your own business or are a freelancer, make sure you create a written contract for each project or new client. When you do so, both parties know what is expected and nothing gets lost in translation. Seeing the terms in writing also allows you an opportunity to ask questions or negotiate the details.

This is also a great tactic when you're hoping to get noticed at work. Try taking notes and documenting any ideas you share during team brainstorming. It's a great a reminder of your contributions, which is particularly useful if your concept is incorporated into the new proposal that ultimately wins the business. Jessica and her team create a quarterly memo in which they set and track their goals throughout the year; it also enables them to be ready when one of the magazines or higher-ups asks for a recap of their efforts.

Short-cuts Fall Short

In a world where most people (at least those under 30) write in shorthand because they are almost exclusively e-mailing or text messaging, we can easily forget that using e-mail at work should still be considered business correspondence, as if you were writing a typewritten letter and sending it to an executive or client. Other tips, some of which you may have heard, bear repeating:

- Don't use icons :-) or abbreviations (LOL). You're not in middle school, and electronic communication should be treated as formally as a written memo would be.
- Avoid using all caps or overusing exclamation points, which in texts and e-mails connotes yelling instead of enthusiasm.
- Saying "thank you" and "please" is important. Refrain from abbreviating those words. (They're not that long to begin with!)

◆ ◆ ◆ ◆

"When are you due? Oh, you're not pregnant?"...
and other communication gaffes to avoid at all costs

Even PR people step in it once in a while. Here are some things you can learn from our past experiences:

1. **Never assume *anything* about *anyone*.** You know that old saying, "When you assume, you make an 'ass' out of 'u' and 'me'"? Case in point: We don't care how pregnant a woman looks—*do not* offer your

congratulations on the impending birth of her child unless *she* brings it up first. In general, it's best not to jump to conclusions about someone's marital status, ethnic or religious background, sexual orientation, or the like.

2. **We don't like "like," "you know"?** We've both had young employees who, *like*, peppered their speech with these, *you know*, words so often that we had to, *like*, sit them down and tell them to practice speaking without, *you know*, saying them because no one would, *like*, take them seriously if, *you know*, they sounded like airheads. Whether you use those filler words or empty catch phrases to fill the dead air, it dilutes your message and impacts the level of respect people feel for you and what you have to say. Streamline for the utmost effectiveness.

3. **Avoid calling someone you just met by a nickname...unless they introduce themselves as such.** It irks Jessica to no end when a brand new business acquaintance calls her *Jess*, *Jessie*, or, even worse, *sweetie* or *honey*, without asking her if it's okay. Nicknames connote familiarity and, when you are just starting a professional relationship, you should be a bit more formal and show some respect. Unless a person asks you to call them "Babs" instead of Barbara, refer to them by their given name.

◆ ◆ ◆ ◆

Your Personal PR Action Plan

1. **Perfect your elevator pitch.** Whether for a new job, a promotion, a business idea, or a pitch for a freelance assignment, write down everything you want to get across. Don't try to start with a pithy statement—free write for three pages without stopping, editing, or spell-checking. Pretend you're

trapped in an actual elevator with the ideal person you'd like to pitch—the president of a company you'd love to work for, a dream client, someone you'd want as a mentor, a potential investor, etc.

- What would you say to them in the 30 seconds the elevator is stuck between floors to convince them to listen to you and hire you?
- What can you offer that's unique?
- What are you "selling"?
- What's your ultimate goal?
- Why should they hear you out?

2. Once you've jotted down answers to these questions, hone your message down to a few punchy sentences and then read them aloud in a confident voice. Would you be wowed?

3. Next, use the same information to prepare your press release. What is the most timely piece of news? What would your headline be? What are the five Ws that need to be communicated?

Chapter 2

Always Have a Plan (and a Back-Up Plan)

"A goal without a plan is just a wish."
—*Antoine de Saint-Exupery*

Whether we're looking to land a big story, get our client on television, help shape someone's image, or pull off an event, before we do anything, we start with a PR plan. Why? Because a plan creates a roadmap for success and provides a lens through which all communication is seen. Without one, publicity could just be random pitches and words, adrift, like a boat without a rudder. If you're trying to get a job, earn recognition in your current position, or build your business or professional image, you need to build a plan that will help guide the way to your end goal.

 Sound Bite

"By failing to prepare, you are preparing to fail."
—Benjamin Franklin

Begin With the End Game

In Lewis Carroll's *Alice's Adventures in Wonderland,* Alice asks The Cheshire Cat where she ought to go from there and the Cat responds, "That depends a good deal on where you want to get to." When Alice replies, "I don't much care where," the Cat says, "Then it doesn't much matter which way you go."

When playing chess, the end-game strategy basically means focusing on the win and working backwards to achieve it. In PR, as in all business, it's about defining what winning the "game" means (in other words, what your dream outcome is) and then working toward it. If you are in a job, your particular end game could be that title change, raise, or even being allowed to hire that much-needed person for the team. If you are a consultant, perhaps it is winning that client or executing a job that you've been hired to do.

How many of us have had to endure meetings, only to walk out without having addressed the primary reason for the gathering in the first place? Time management expert Julie Morgenstern advises her clients not to attend any meeting that doesn't have an agenda or a clear set of goals. It works, too. Since Jessica started implementing that rule, she has saved herself from endless hours of meetings where nothing gets done. She says to start by asking, "What are we trying to accomplish here? What will move the needle for the situation and what is the news? These simple questions help you understand what you need to communicate and who it needs to be communicated to."

Self-help guru Anthony Robbins advocates: What you focus on, you move toward—whether you're talking about your career, or, for example, racecar driving. In the latter, look toward the wall, and you will crash into it. But look around the curve, and that's where you'll head. With your career—instead of worrying about the challenging economy or trouble with a boss—focusing on a successful resolution will help you navigate the tough times more effectively than focusing on the bad things that could happen someday. Once you know where you want to end up, you can build your objectives—that is, what you want to accomplish.

News Flash:
Tailor your plan

We asked Beth Thomas Cohen, president and partner at B'squared Public Relations, how she goes about building a PR plan for her fashion clients:

"First, I always look at the brand or designer I am representing to see where they would typically sit—Where in a store? In what magazines? Next to which designers?

It's important to lay out goals you feel are obtainable and some things you would like to reach for. Make sure that each plan is catered to each client, as everyone's agenda and approach should differ in some way. Create a formal strategy and then hit the ground running. Determine how you will announce this. Who will be interested in what we are showing them? Who is the consumer? The best target market? These are the first questions you need to address."

The Takeaway: Get clear on what you want to accomplish and then determine who might be interested. If you're a consultant and you want to generate, new business, start by thinking about what revenue numbers you'd like to generate or the kinds of business you're hoping to acquire. If you're at a job, is your objective a raise? A promotion? More flextime? Break down your objectives into small steps and, as Thomas Cohen says, "hit the ground running."

How Do You Get There?

Whether your goal is as simple as making a new contact, or as complex and time-intensive as changing perceptions about a product or person, you must first set objectives. Start by asking yourself what you want to achieve:

- Are you looking to build awareness for a new product or service—or yourself?

- Are you angling for a raise, recognition, or promotion?
- Are you trying to win a new client or project?
- What is your dream job or opportunity?

Now that you know where you want to go, what are the broad strokes for how you'll get there? In public relations, there are tried-and-true methods, typically falling in categories from baseline pitching to one-on-one meetings, strategic partnerships, and stunts.

Baseline pitching

Public relations hinges on the pitch—a punchy, succinct message that simultaneously tells a story and piques the interest of the audience. In PR, the audience is typically the media, the consumer, or another business. For a job hunter, the audience is the HR person or potential boss. For a person hoping for a promotion, the target could be your company CEO or the person to whom you report.

Michael Volpatt of boutique PR agency Larkin/Volpatt Communications cites planned and specific outreach as a key element of success. "Getting a job, or in the case of my business partner and me getting new clients, is all about calculated outreach. Successful PR people know that you have to reach out to reporters—and when you reach out in a calculated way, it often results in success (in the form of placements, briefings, and respect for your strategic process)." Jayne Wallace, vice president of corporate communications for Virgin Mobile USA, agrees. "Solid stories don't need to be over-the-top creative if you've answered the question for the reporter, 'Why should I care?' Ultimately, most great hits have come from strong stories/trends." Likewise, when you are pitching your personal story, you should ask yourself, "Why should a potential employer/client/business partner care? What exactly can I bring to the table?"

Face-to-face/one-on-one meetings

In building a PR plan, we often look for ways to get the brand spokesperson in front of the right media and right influencers, as it's been proven to be one of the most effective ways to make an impact. Meryl's longtime client, Dale Carnegie Training, recently ran an ad campaign carrying the "Get Human" concept, the gist of which was: *Nothing trumps face-to-face interpersonal interaction when you are trying to sell an idea or get resolution on an issue.* This is true in any field, according to Dana Fields Muldrow, senior manager of national public relations for a large professional services firm. "In today's technology-driven world, it easy to forget about the personal touch. Shooting off a quick e-mail, sending a text message, or leaving a voice mail enables us to hide our true selves. We can say and do things in the digital universe that can be misunderstood, misdirected, and misconstrued. That's a lot of misses! While it may seem old school to have a live telephone conversation, meet in person, or send a handwritten note, sometimes they are the best forms of communication and the only way people (your clients, reporters, etc.) may ever get to really know and ultimately trust you."

That theory is supported by a report created by *Forbes Insights* ("Business Meetings: The Case for Face to Face," 2009), in which executives still expressed an overwhelming preference for face-to-face meetings, with more than eight out of 10 saying they prefer in-person contact to virtual communication. And, for those who favored in-person interactions, they believed that face-to-face meetings were essential in building stronger, more meaningful relationships (85 percent) and greater social interaction (75 percent).

Mailings/creative deliveries

A breakthrough delivery can often help you get noticed by someone whose attention is pulled in numerous directions every day. When representing liquor brands, which Meryl has been doing for many years, it often helps to actually send out the product—along with a clever card or knick-knack—on a quarterly basis. That way, when a media person is writing a story that your—let's say vodka brand—can fit into, he or she will think of your brand for the story. The same holds true if you're a consultant vying for a project, or a job-seeker looking for your next gig. That creatively designed resume or impeccably created corporate brochure will land on a desk and stand out from the crowd.

You might be rolling your eyes, thinking that you don't want to add more clutter to the world; we don't blame you. Instead, we recommend making something that ties into or is an extension of your personal brand. For example:

- As a consultant or small-business owner, perhaps you need to create a brochure or giveaway to keep your services top-of-mind.
- Looking for a job? It could be as simple as a creatively designed calling card or personal Website.
- If you are in a job but looking to stand out, finding ways to showcase what you do—such as a well-organized project report, handwritten note, or even strategically timed internal recap e-mail—could make the difference.

Frankly, the creative "delivery" could even be you—in other words, how you present yourself in the workplace. We'll cover appearance more in depth in Chapter 6, but sometimes a simple tweak to your wardrobe or appearance could go a long way to getting noticed in the workplace.

Stunts

A publicity stunt is a planned, often large-scale event designed to attract the public's attention and garner media coverage.

And, over the years, we have been part of our fair share of stunts—everything from hiring presidential impersonators to launch a hotel, to building the world's largest glass of iced tea, to getting the first live horse on the floor of the New York Stock Exchange. But you don't have to be a big brand—or have a big budget—to launch a creative stunt of your own. According to *PRWeek*, when MIT graduate Joshua Persky couldn't find a job as a finance engineer, he hit the street—literally. He donned a sandwich board, passed out resumes, and basically hawked himself for a job in New York city. What followed was significant publicity with a global reach, tons of well wishers, a significant following for his blog—jonathanpersky.com. And, oh yes—a job.

News Flash:
Tap the zeitgeist

Joshua Persky shares how he inadvertently became the face of the current recession—and became famous in Korea:

"It wasn't my initial aim to be in the news—it's really hard to plan going viral. I simply wanted to hand out resumes and for people to know what I was doing. So, in June of 2008, I put on a signboard reading 'Experienced MIT Graduate for Hire' and my wife sent a photograph of me wearing it to local papers. A story ran in the *New York Observer* and the *New York Daily News* one day. Within the week, my story had run in the media all around the world. I even got a call from friends that saw the story in Korea! My phone rang off the hook for months and tons of new leads were generated.

Ultimately, it did lead to me getting a career coach whose advice, in turn, led to two job opportunities. It also opened up a world of opportunities with my blog, speaking engagements, and entrepreneurial pursuits."

The Takeaway: Stunts are most effective when they are tied to current trends and are both bold and unique.

Endorsements

In PR, celebrity sells—both literally and figuratively. Think about how products fly off the shelves once they've been featured on the fabulous Ms. Oprah Winfrey's "O List." While Oprah is the Holy Grail of celebrity endorsement, even a lesser-known name can help raise awareness for a brand, event, or another person. Then there's also the implied endorsement of a high-profile person. PR people leverage celebrities' comings and goings, what they wear and drink, to raise awareness for their clients. (Think about the mileage that retailers such as J. Crew are getting out of Michelle Obama's clothing choices!) If people read about it in *Us Weekly* or see it on *Access Hollywood*, maybe they'll want to jump on the bandwagon, too.

Steve Dumain, founder and creative director of luxury accessory brand Be & D, discovered this firsthand after launching the company's handbags at Bergdorf Goodman. When pictures of A-list celebrities carrying their "Garbo" and "Crawford" bags began to crop up all over the press, Dumain says, "It changed everything and the sales went crazy. Neiman Marcus, Saks, and the hot little boutiques called to carry our brand. We were in celebrity weeklies right away so everyone knew our bag…. Our revenues grew exponentially."

While we're not saying that you need someone of Oprah's caliber to get ahead or get noticed, it is good to think about who can support and vouch for you in your workplace and in the industry. For example, you could ask former employers, colleagues, and clients to recommend you on the professional networking site LinkedIn or send a note of praise about you to someone you're interested in meeting. If you have your own business, ask clients to give you testimonials about the great work you've done to include on your Website. Media trainer Joyce Newman says, "When you're being your best publicist, ask people to put their thank yous and feedback in writing so you can use it as a testimonial. It's [also] really helpful when someone tells three other people what a good job you did."

Sound Bite

"If you don't have a plan for yourself, you'll be a part of someone else's."
—American proverb

Time Is of the Essence

Public relations is all about timing. Working with deadline-pressed media, we must get news out before it leaks, and we have to constantly orchestrate when a plan should be executed for maximum effect. But timing can be important for anyone, particularly when trying to achieve a goal. Once you've decided what you want and chosen some key strategies, we recommend establishing a specific end date, even if the project doesn't have a preordained hard stop. You can always readjust, but having a target day and/or time will help create a sense of urgency to keep things moving towards the finish line.

Meryl's sister has a blog, 500x50.com, which outlines personal and professional goals that she wants to accomplish before 50. Some are easy ("Don't watch TV for a month"); some are more difficult to accomplish ("Be conversational in Arabic"). She knows that ticking off everything would be impossible, even if she dedicated 24/7 to doing so, having a looming deadline (however far down the road it may be) drives her to maximize her free time and strive to accomplish as many of the line items as she can prior to entering her sixth decade.

Even if you're not dealing with a news window or a fast-approaching birthday, establishing timeframes for your personal and professional goals keeps you focused and moving forward. Working backwards from the deadline, break down the tasks into bite-sized pieces. It's like being on a diet: if you say, "I'm going to drop 20 pounds in the next month, cut out all fat and exercise six times a week," by day three, you'll likely have fallen off the wagon. If you gradually add healthy habits or small tasks into your everyday routine—whether it's switching to skim milk or making three cold calls—you'll be much more likely to accomplish your ultimate goal. Monitor your progress regularly and adjust as you go along to ensure you're on track. And, as you develop your timeline, don't forget to build in wiggle room in the event you hit a roadblock.

Beer or Champagne Budget?

As we all know, nothing in life is free and with almost any plan comes a budget—the literal cost of doing business. As PR is not a directly revenue-producing industry, we have to map out and use our budgets wisely. It's easy to see the applications when you are creating something–a resume, a presentation, an event. But you should also be considering time, energy, and intellectual capital as you are setting the budget for any project. Consultants already have this mindset, but it's smart of employees to consider what their hourly rate might be and take that to heart when planning or executing any efforts. Clearly, if you're looking to get a loan or be paid by a client, most projects won't get green-lighted without some sort of projected budget in place. Those looking for a job should consider the costs of building a Website, buying a new suit, printing copies of a resume, or paying for grooming services like a haircut or manicure when setting a budget.

We start by looking at what it will take to get things done: time, resources (or people), and actual money outlay. Are you setting up an office? There will be rent to pay, equipment to acquire, paper clips to buy. Are you hosting a party? Don't forget costs for incidentals including wait staff, ice, gift bags, etc.

Be prepared for the inevitable hidden or unexpected costs that arise. Of course, if you get to your goal with a little extra money left over at the end, you can buy yourself a glass of champagne to toast the accomplishment!

 Key Message:
Be frugal

Steve Dumain, entrepreneur and founder of Be & D, offers the following advice about expenditures:

"Never ever spend another penny until you need to. The thing that really saved us [when we were starting out] and stretched us as long as possible was not spending where we didn't need it. We did it guerilla style. For example, business cards weren't an option for two years. We told people we forgot them and sent e-mails instead....You have to be resourceful."

The Back-up Plan

In the 1970s song, "Fifty Ways to Leave Your Lover," Paul Simon has not one, but 49 back-up plans in his pocket to extricate himself from the "situation." Even in driver's ed, you learn basic defensive driving: always have an escape route.

Savvy companies have a contingency plan, and all smart PR people have a few tricks up their sleeves. You should always have a Plan B (and C and D).

Mapping out as many "Doomsday scenarios" in advance will help you prepare for an unexpected storm. Start by making a list of all things that could go wrong on a particular project. Then, come up with ways to counter those in a timely manner. Hosting an event outdoors? Have a tent at the ready. Big presentation not loading on your laptop? Bring a back-up on a USB port. Internet goes down right as you have to do a big e-mail blast? Go use the free WiFi at Starbucks or Barnes & Noble.

Years ago, at a management conference for Jessica's company, the musician her group had hired up and quit in the middle of his performance (he was upset that the conference attendees were using castanets and maracas that had been handed out instead of paying attention to his Flamenco guitar playing). Luckily, the events team had booked a DJ for later that evening and had him start spinning immediately so guests could continue dancing. If they hadn't thought of a back-up plan, the evening's festivities would have been a bust.

The same holds true when you're pitching a story—or your business—says Melissa Hobley, chief marketing officer of Buyology, Inc.: "You need to be able to be on the phone with someone and when they pass on your first idea, you need to have five others on deck, whether looking for a job, a story, etc."

Hopefully, your "back-up" exercise will remain just that, but if the worst-case scenario becomes reality, you'll be relieved that there is already a plan in place. Remember, in the immortal words of author (and famed cardinal) Richard James Cushing, it's important to "Always plan ahead. It wasn't raining when Noah built the ark."

News Flash:
Rules are made to be broken,
so don't be afraid to "hop the fence"

Some rules are absolutely meant to be followed: Eat your vegetables. Do unto others as you would have them to do unto you. Don't run with scissors. That said, there are times when a quick-end run around the status quo is just what's needed to stand out and get where you need to go.

Meryl recalls one such experience during a work trip to Las Vegas, where she and her team were putting in long hours at the Palms Hotel during the MTV Music Awards. Given the crowds, navigating a route to their client's suite was quite challenging. Roadblocks and throngs of people soon made it clear that there had to be a better way. The cab transporting the team had gotten about as close as it could to the spot, but thanks to barricades and barriers put up for crowd control, it was still a good, long walk in heels if they followed the designated path to the hotel.

But Meryl's colleague saw an opportunity—a low fence that allowed for a shortcut right to the door–and the rest of the group followed suit, allowing them to reach their destination quickly.

The Takeaway: It's important to look for ways to streamline the process—the shortest distance between two points, even if it means breaking the rules a bit. Sometimes being the first to hop the proverbial fence means spending less time maneuvering and more time getting the job done.

Check Yourself

After all is said and done, compiling an overview of key learnings can help increase effectiveness. These kinds of case studies will give you a powerful tool when negotiating for a raise, lobbying for a new client, or vying for a new job. Ask yourself:

- Have you reached your desired destination or goal? If not, how do you adjust accordingly?
- Did you give yourself a realistic timeframe in which to accomplish your goals?
- What worked and what didn't? What lessons did you learn?

 Sound Bite

"I love it when a plan comes together!"
—Colonel John "Hannibal" Smith, *The A-Team*

Under-promising and over-delivering can be difficult, particularly if you are hard-wired to want to impress. Subsequently, over the years, PR people in general have garnered a bad reputation for not being completely forthright about what they could do or deliver.

So, what if things are not going as planned? Delays happen. Roadblocks arise. There's no crime in readjusting. The most important thing is communication–with managers, teammates, clients, etc.; tell them what you think you can realistically deliver and then no one will be surprised. Nobody wants to be blindsided at the eleventh hour.

According to Dianna Booher, author of *The Voice of Authority* (McGraw-Hill, June 2007), if it's bad news, tell it promptly: "Never underestimate the importance of the two-minute warning—without the two-minute warning in a ball game, the trailing team may miss their chance to redouble their efforts to catch up before they lose." Shawn Sachs, CEO of PR firm Sunshine Sachs & Associates adds, "Be honest, whether with the media or with your clients. I'm a big fan of being in front of things. The psychology of any issue—it's what your parents told you when you were kids—is it'll only get worse. Sooner or later you'll get busted, so be up-front."

Sound Bite

"Strategy without tactics is the slowest route to victory. Tactics without strategy is the noise before defeat."
—Sun Tsu

Forget the phrase "I don't know" ...and other tricks to build your plan

With curveballs flying and roads diverging all over the place, success hinges on resourcefulness. Some other tips we've learned along the way include:

- **Forget the phrase "I don't know."** In this day and age, there really is no excuse for this response. If you don't know something, find out! Look it up online. Ask someone to help you. Read a book. If you come up against a problem, big or small, you must do everything in your power to find a solution, a chink in the armor, a passage across the impermeable. This means utilizing technology, connections, common sense, and plain old elbow grease (thanks, Grandpa!) to get things done. We agree with the old saying, "Anything worth having is worth working for."

- **Be audacious.** You get what you settle for in life. So, if you think big and strive for lofty goals, chances are, you'll get close if not completely there. As outlined in Tilar J. Mazzeo's book, The Widow Clicquot: The Story of a Champagne Empire and the Woman Who Ruled It, Barbe-Nicole Clicquot Ponsardin (The Widow Clicquot) was a 19th-century entrepreneur whose innovative champagne-making methods are still used today. Widowed at the age of 27, she bucked tradition by stepping in to run her husband's then modest wine business—ultimately building what is now one of the best-known Champagne brands around. How did she do this? Pure audacity; by not letting setbacks derail her, she not only succeeded, but thrived in a time when women were little more than second-class citizens.

  PR agency owner Heidi Krupp used her own self-starter personality to get noticed when she was just a lowly assistant to Barbara Walters' PR person. "We were working on her *Most Fascinating People* special, I came up with a public relations strategy on my own and showed it to Barbara, who was impressed and asked me to do the publicity for the special. It ended up being an amazing experience and a career opportunity for me. In addition to giving me my first publicity credit, it gave me confidence in knowing that I could figure out a strategy for publicity and come up with interesting new ideas. When I left 20/20, one of the things that Ms. Walters said to me before I left was, 'As a publicist, you have to look at yourself in the mirror and believe in what you're pitching and be able to go to sleep at night knowing that you were true to you.' I totally hold that true to every project I work on."

- **Learn by example.** There's a famous story in Meryl's family about how she and her twin sister learned to stand up on their own. As the tale goes, Meryl struggled over and over again, pulling herself up in her crib, only to fall back down again. After a full afternoon of watching Meryl attempt to stand, her sister stood up on the first try. PR pro Susan Portnoy advocates "learning by osmosis; identify aspects of colleagues or friends' performances that you admire and emulate. Figure out what makes what they do special and put your own spin on it. Learn from others' mistakes." Sometimes the answer is right in front of you. In PR, we are always using negative or positive real-life examples as case studies to set success guidelines and future strategies.

Your Personal PR Action Plan

1. Start mapping your strategy:
   - Identify your top three objectives.
   - Review the tactics above and determine which you can use to accomplish those goals.
   - Decide which materials or collateral will you want on hand as you work towards your objectives.
   - Set a date to accomplish the goal.
   - Be aware of specific cash or energy outlay. How much money or time do you estimate it will cost you?
2. Consider your Doomsday scenario (a list of all things that could go wrong on a particular project). Come up with a few ways to counter those in a timely manner.

Chapter 3
Be a Know-It-All
(in a Good Way)

"An investment in knowledge pays the best interest."
—*Benjamin Franklin*

Even though our mothers always told us that "nobody likes a know-it-all," we have to disagree. (Sorry, Mom.) Sure, it's true that people who think they know everything—but, in most cases, don't—can be extremely annoying. But we're referring to those who try to learn all there is to know about a particular subject, company, or industry. In public relations, gathering as much information as you can about your clients—what makes them unique, what makes them tick, and who they compete with, for example—is vital in determining the best communications strategy for them. We truly could not do our jobs without that. Why? Because part of being able to pitch and persuade effectively is having extensive knowledge of the subject matter, as well as the person or people receiving that pitch.

And when someone sits in on a meeting, or comes in to interview with us for a position, and has read up on recent news about our company or clients, knows something about us and our background,

51

is familiar with our competition and comes armed with intelligent questions, that's exactly the kind of know-it-all we like.

In this day and age, when you can get all the information you need in a few keystrokes, we're amazed at how many people walk into a meeting without any preparation. Trust us, it shows. Personally, we would never get together with a reporter for the first time, even just for a friendly meet-and-greet, without reading his or her latest articles and researching the outlet for which he or she writes. We want to know: What kinds of stories does this person cover? Has he written about our company or our competition? Does he have a style or a particular angle that comes through? Is he fair and fact-based, or snarky and opinionated? How long has she been on the beat? Where was she before? How knowledgeable is she about our business?

We recommend approaching every interaction this way. A guiding principle of PR: Strive to know as much, if not more than, the person with whom you're meeting or speaking; it's the best way to feel comfortable, whatever situation you are walking into.

Key Message:
Become the ultimate expert

Media trainer Joyce Newman shared advice on becoming a "know-it-all": "The best advice I received was from Ed Bernays, the father of PR, who said, 'Joyce, if you ever want to be perceived as an expert at something, you need to query or poll 25 other experts on the subject and ask them to give you 200 words or less on a particular topic for an article or speech and then write about what they said, but you get to give the defining point and come across as the über-expert.'"

Sound Bite

"Most of the successful people I've known are the ones who do more listening than talking."
—Bernard M. Baruch,
American economist

First, Know Thyself

One of the most important things to do before pursuing a professional goal is to do a "soul search" before the job search, as career coach Maggie Mistal puts it. She adds, "It's important to clarify who you are [and what] your core genius [is]. Too many people try to shoehorn themselves into what's out there. Instead, if you get clear on your unique set of strengths and interests, you'll be better equipped to differentiate yourself in a crowded marketplace."

Social media guru and founder of Help A Reporter Out (HARO) Peter Shankman agrees: "Everyone is an expert at something—even if he or she is an expert at *Seinfeld* and can quote lines from the show backward and forward. The trick is to understand what makes you an expert and try to leverage that to highlight your uniqueness." How can you do that? Buyology's Melissa Hobley says it's as simple as asking other people what makes you great—why are you a great friend, employee, volunteer. You'll be surprised at the responses (hopefully pleasantly!).

Key Message:
Find your purpose; follow your distinct path

According to Maggie Mistal, "Each one of us has a distinct purpose. The minute you get clear about what that is, you can position yourself in the right industries and produce extraordinary results. It is actually easier, because it comes naturally to you."

Go on a Research Mission

Jessica once asked a candidate interviewing for a position on her staff, "So what's your favorite magazine in our stable?" "*Glamour*," the woman answered. While it's a perfectly good magazine, *Glamour* is published by Hearst's biggest competitor, Condé Nast. The fact that this woman didn't familiarize herself with the titles Hearst Magazines publishes before interviewing at the company immediately knocked her out of the running. Lesson: Never go in cold to an interview or business meeting. Arming yourself with knowledge will make you smarter, more confident, and more appealing to the person on the other end, whether a potential client or employer.

When a brand-new media beat reporter started at the *New York Times*, Jessica researched his background before reaching out to set up a meeting and discovered that they had gone to the same college (although not at the same time). She ended her introductory note to him with a "Go Blue!"—The University of Michigan's well-known cheer—and it created an instant connection. He responded immediately, and they went on to collaborate on several stories.

Sheila Munguia, president of P. Public Relations, who worked at a major beauty company for many years, told us how doing research helped her land a job there. "Getting an interview was a big opportunity, and I knew this was my one shot. I went into my first interview (and another subsequent six interviews with top executives) knowing this was my moment to shine. I did extensive research, prepared examples of great work I had executed, polished up my clip book—I was prepared to pitch myself from every possible angle and demonstrate how well I knew this company's business. All that homework paid off because my first interview was the toughest interview I have ever experienced, and I got the job."

TODAY Show Producer Sarah Clagett recalls a pitch that could have been made better with a little bit of knowledge. A deluge of pitches from PR people flood into Sarah's inbox on a daily basis. To grab her attention, the e-mail must pique her interest. An unabashed college basketball fan, Sarah was pleased to see a pitch come in about March Madness and connected with the publicist immediately. The PR girl, though, seemed surprised that Sarah was so excited about the pitch. While she booked the segment, Sarah's perception of the publicist was significantly affected. She pointed out, "A simple search would have likely uncovered my passion and that would have helped build a connection. On the flip side, doing research about my interests or other topics that I've covered would prevent her from pitching things that wouldn't interest me, saving time, money and effort—both hers and mine."

Given how easy it is to access information today, there is *no* excuse for not doing your research.

"Google is a verb for a reason"
...and other resources to find any information
you need to get up to speed

PR people know that they must come "packing" to any meeting, interview or cocktail party; they must be armed with information to help drive the conversation and make their point. Here are some resources—both well-known and obscure—to help:

- **Search for it.** Nowadays, you can find everything from books to maps to images and government records simply by finding the right link. Consider tapping the electronic catalogs from your local university or public library as additional reliable resources. Of course, as most of us already know, the easiest—and most pervasive—way to research something quickly is to type it into the search bar on Google and see what comes up. One of the top results will likely be Wikipedia.org, "a multilingual, Web-based, free-content encyclopedia project based on an openly editable model" that enables you to find the most updated information on pretty much anything under the sun. Unlike the hefty volumes of the *Encyclopedia Brittanica* that we grew up with (and were outdated almost before they finished printing the current edition), Wikipedia is easy to use, accessible from anywhere and—most uniquely—editable by anyone who has knowledge on a particular subject (although there are checks and balances in place to make sure the information is as accurate as possible and no one is abusing the right to contribute). Because the information available is controlled by an ever-changing community, beware of taking what you read as gospel because it may not all be accurate. It's a very good resource if you don't rely on it exclusively.

- **Listen up.** Another great way to track the latest buzz and news online is to sign up for an online news feeder or aggregator service, which will pull relevant information about your topics of interest from all over the Web and put them on one page. Most people know about Google Alerts, but there are tons of other resources to tap when setting up the RSS feeds and other monitoring efforts. Check Twitter and other social media sites to be sure you're up on the most current information. We'll talk a bit more about setting up an online listening post in Chapter 9.

- **Consume media.** There's still a lot to be said for traditional media resources like magazines, newspapers, and books. In fact, mediabistro's Laurel Touby strongly suggests reading the *Wall Street Journal* and the *New York Times* cover to cover every day to provide fodder for any conversation you may have, personal or professional. If that's too "old school," go to your local newspaper's Website or an outlet like CNN.com, and check out the day's news. You can also go to the bookstore or library: whatever industry you are in (or would like to be), there are tons of resources and references available that will give you a crash course on what you need to know. For example, if you're interviewing at Sotheby's, a wealth of books are available on the history of the venerable auction house (as well as its competitors, such as Christie's). Get your hands on catalogs from past auctions to see what kinds of art and relics they've represented. Read magazines such as *Art & Auction* and *Art & Antiques* to stay up-to-date on trends in that world. If you're vying for a job in investment banking, make *Investor's Business Daily*, *The Wall Street Journal*, *Barron's* and *Financial Times* part of your regular reading. In addition, read well-known books about the industry, such as *Liar's Poker* and *The Big Short: Inside the Doomsday Machine* by Michael Lewis, *Too Big to Fail* by Andrew Ross Sorkin, and *On the Brink* by Henry M. Paulson.

Spin the Web

In the Internet era, finding information is as simple as a click of the mouse. Though it's important to make sure you're going to legitimate outlets (newspaper sites, credible blogs, and online sources), you can track down everything from the latest news and gossip—although we would caution against believing every rumor that runs online—to company profiles and executive bios quickly and easily on the Internet. Don't eschew the power of print either; we recommend reading the appropriate newspapers and magazines that cover what's going on in your area of interest. For example, if you're dying for a job in fashion, in addition to following fashion industry blogs like *Fashionista*, *Fashionologie*, and *Fashion Week Daily*, we would suggest reading the Thursday and Sunday "Styles" section of the *New York Times*, the fashion trade *WWD*, as well as all the major fashion magazines (*Harper's Bazaar*, *ELLE*, *Vogue*, *W*) so you are up on the latest news and trend information, from all different resources, on what's in and what's out. Don't know the key trades? Google or check out Twitter to find a starting point.

If you're interviewing at a company for a position, freelance assignment, or to be a vendor, check out its Website. Most companies these days have a site with their latest news, executive bios, and client list or brand information (if not, they should!). If you're seeking a job, many of them also list open positions—although we find that there are often better ways to land an interview or job than going through human resources. Why anyone would go on an interview without having checked out a company's site to gather easily accessible information on its business is beyond comprehension; but, alas, many people skip that simple step. To us, it's a big red flag that the person is not resourceful or simply uninterested in landing the job or assignment.

In addition, social media sites can be very helpful. Use Twitter to follow people in your industry, media who cover it, or those who work at the company at which you're interviewing. For example, we know someone in advertising who saw a post on Twitter from the chief creative officer of a great agency looking to hire new creative talent. Our friend immediately e-mailed his resume and landed an interview. Had he not been tracking his industry on social media, he would never have known this agency was hiring. In short, check your Twitter feeds and lists before any meeting or media interview.

If you have time, set up a Google alert for the company you're pitching and track their online coverage in the week or two before your meeting. You can also try to hook up with industry folks on Facebook and LinkedIn, although there's no guarantee that they'll accept your invite if they don't know you. However, if you have a friend or colleague in common, it helps to mention that when you ask them to connect with you.

 Sound Bite

"When I was first starting out, I was told: 'Information is currency; don't be caught counterfeiting.'"
—Matthew Hiltzik,
president & CEO of Hiltzik Strategies, LLC

Study Your Competition

Just as important as researching the place you're trying to work is studying its competitive landscape. Companies and brands shouldn't operate in a vacuum, and neither should you. The most successful people are aware of what their rivals are doing so they can determine how to be better and more innovative in order to stay ahead of the curve. The best PR people are constantly monitoring the news for what their clients' or company's competitors are up to, what kind of press they're getting, and what new products or ideas are happening in their industry. When looking for a job, you should track not only the companies where you're interviewing, but also their top competitors. By 7:30 a.m. every morning, Jessica's entire team receives an e-mail round-up of the morning's media industry news so they are not only aware of what press their own company has received, but also that of their competitors. All PR folks know the value of reading the day's headlines to get a snapshot of what's being talked about. If you don't know what's going on, how can you leverage it?

Want that promotion? Pitching new business? Pay attention to who the other contenders might be. Here are some specific examples:

- If you're in office supply sales, find out what your competitors are charging before you meet with a potential buyer. Are their prices more competitive? How does their customer service compare to yours? Do they have a better selection?
- If interviewing for a job at a Website, spend time not only on their site, but competitive sites as well. How are they different? What do they each do well? Is their format and design user-friendly? Do they give "link love" to the right sites and bloggers?

- If you're planning to open a restaurant, check out the best places in the neighborhood you're considering. What kind of cuisine do they serve? Are they casual or fancy? What are the price points? Are they busy? What does the clientele look like? Will your establishment offer something unique?

Conduct your own informal focus group. Ask friends and family about their impressions of each company or brand in the category so you can go in prepared with anecdotal research on what people are looking for.

Key Message: Diversify

According to PR pro Susan Portnoy, "Don't over-focus your skills. Do your best to understand the ebb and flow of PR for a variety of industries. Understand all the media in which your story can be told. Stay current and embrace new technologies. The more you are able to tackle successfully, the more valuable you will be to a larger group of individuals, companies, and clients."

Survey the Lay of the Land

Years ago, a friend of ours just starting out in the advertising business landed an interview at a big agency. Having been trained to dress up for a job interview, he showed up in a suit and tie and immediately realized his wardrobe choice had been a mistake. Things have definitely changed since the days of *Mad Men*: everyone in the office was in jeans and sneakers. Not only did our pal feel completely out of place, but he also sent the message to those he met with that he didn't do his research. He did not get the job there, but having learned more about the industry's creative, casual environment, he nailed his *next* interview (dressed in less formal attire) and was hired at an even better agency.

Before you go in for a meeting somewhere, find out about the vibe of the company. If possible, interview people who work at the company or have done business with them or their employees. What do they like and dislike about it? What's the corporate culture? Is it a traditional or cutting-edge place? Does the company have a collaborative, open floor plan with no private offices? Do they typically make decisions quickly or slowly? Are employees expected to wear suits or is more casual attire allowed?

Where is their office located? Even for something as simple as that, you want to make sure you leave yourself enough time to arrive at your appointment promptly. Figure out the best way to get there; then do a dry run to see how long it takes. There's nothing worse than running late for an interview or new business pitch and arriving sweaty and distracted. You want to get there at least 5-10 minutes early so you have time to collect yourself, go over your messages and notes, or use the restroom. On the flip side: Don't arrive more than 15 minutes early—getting there too far in advance of your appointment can inconvenience the person with whom you're scheduled to meet and leave you too much time to work up your nerves in the waiting room.

 Sound Bite

"Be prepared. It's like being a lawyer—you have to know your defendant's argument better than they do. That's what I learned in law school."
—Alison Schwartz Dorfman, producer, *CBS Evening News*

Cultivate Your Figure-it-out Gene

In this era of smaller staffs and employees taking on more responsibility than ever before, managers and clients have less time to micromanage and teach people how to do every little thing. An industry colleague once told a staffer who came to her stymied by a situation and at a standstill, "If I were in your place, instead of coming to my boss or client, I would rather call 311, 411, my mother, my grandmother, my best friend, my priest, my college professor, my cousin, or my mail carrier before throwing in the towel." In other words, use your figure-it-out gene. Be your own best publicist by trying to learn how to do something before asking for help.

Jessica always tells her staff, "Don't just come to me with a problem. Come to me with at least one potential solution to that problem." It's easy to be lazy and let someone else give you the answers, but you'll go much further if you demonstrate your capacity to solve issues or come up with ideas on your own. We're always impressed when, unsolicited, one of our direct reports comes up with an innovative idea or a new and better way of getting a project done. It shows initiative, thoughtfulness, and a thirst for knowledge—all of which make that person valuable and make our jobs easier.

For example, one of our colleagues figured out a way to send e-mails and press releases to an entire media list at the same time through an automatic, low-cost, online service called MailChimp. When we need to issue an announcement at 7a.m., we no longer need a human being to come into the office at the crack of dawn to manually e-mail every person on our list. This person knew that offering up this resource to the whole team would enable us to work more efficiently and, for that, we were all appreciative.

Some questions to ask yourself before seeking assistance elsewhere:

- What's the best way to achieve my goal on this project/assignment?
- If the obvious way doesn't work, are there alternative methods of getting there?
- Are there new technologies or services available that can help me get the job done faster and more effectively?

- Who else, other than my boss (or client), can I ask for help or ideas?
- Can I learn how to do this task online, from a book/DVD/how-to video or by observing someone else doing it?
- What new ideas can I offer to my boss, colleagues, clients, or company that will be seen as useful, productive, and innovative?

 Sound Bite

"Now you know...and knowing is half the battle."
—G.I. Joe

Fake It 'til You Make It

Big deal if you don't know it all. Who does? In most cases, if you act like you know what you're talking about, people will believe that you do. Now, we're not telling you to make stuff up. If you're asked to give a lecture on quantum physics and don't have a clue what particle/wave duality is (we don't either), that's a different story. But if you have even a little experience in the subject matter, can learn quickly, do your research, and show confidence, there's no reason why you can't convince others that you have a handle on the topic at hand.

If you ever saw a movie called *Working Girl* from the late 1980s, Melanie Griffith stars as a poufy-haired, gum-smacking Wall Street secretary who pretends she's an executive while her boss is in the hospital in order to pitch an idea that she had suggested to her superior. She changes her hair, makeup, and wardrobe into a sleeker, more professional look; learns what she can about mergers and acquisitions; and proceeds to hook up (both professionally and personally) with Harrison Ford's character to broker a major deal to buy a radio network. Okay, so that's pure fiction, but the point is: she did her research, looked the part, acted the part and, more importantly, believed in herself, her ideas, and her abilities. As a result, others ultimately did too—even after her true identity was revealed.

News Flash:
Experience isn't always required

Alec Brownstein, copywriter at Young & Rubicam New York, a big advertising agency, tells us about how self-confidence is sometimes more important than experience:

"I got my first job in advertising with absolutely no prior experience in the industry. Everyone told me that I couldn't get a job as a copywriter without a portfolio of ads. In fact, at my first agency, they hadn't hired a copywriter without a portfolio in [more than] a decade. But I wasn't dissuaded. Rather than give up when they first said no, I convinced them to let me intern for free. I believed strongly that I could come up with ideas for ads, and once I was in the door, I would tell that to anyone who would listen. Eventually, I ended up in front of the right person who gave me the chance to prove myself. Luckily, I didn't disappoint her. But I never would have had that opportunity if I hadn't been willing to be my own publicist."

The Takeaway: Believe in your ability to succeed, even if you don't have a ton of experience—and keep at it until you can prove yourself.

Your Personal PR Action Plan

Take an hour to research the industry or company you're most interested in, whether online, at the library, bookstore, or by interviewing people familiar with it. Try to answer the following:

- What most interests you about it?
- What is its history?
- How it is different from others?
- Why is it a good fit for you?

- How has the industry/company and its notable personalities been covered recently in the news?
- Who are the key players and what are their accomplishments?
- What are three things you didn't know about it previously?
- If someone asked you what you liked most about said industry/company, what would you say?

PROJECT

"Begin somewhere.
You cannot build a reputation
on what you intend to do."
—Liz Smith

Chapter 4
It's All About Who You Know (and Who Knows You)

"No man is an island."
—*John Donne*

"Don't you know who I am?" If we had a dollar for every time someone said that to us, we'd be rich. When it comes to publicity, red carpets and event check-ins tend to draw the type of people who expect to be recognized and treated accordingly. For a moment, let's put aside that it's simply bad form to ask others that question (it either makes the situation uncomfortable or makes you look like a jerk). Instead, for this conversation only, we recommend you examine how others might answer that question if it were coming from you.

Building a strong network and cultivating those personal connections is a key element of success in any industry. But in PR, it's absolutely essential—the fact is, we're really only as good as our contacts. For example:

- Securing a news story hinges on relationships with producers or reporters.

- Attracting the right attendees to an event rises and falls on connecting with the right social contacts.
- Gaining new clients or projects often comes through the word-of-mouth you get from the people you know.
- Having a mentor or champion inside a company—someone who knows you and the work you do—will help you get that plum assignment or help push for your raise and promotion.

Because most opportunities come from both whom you know and who knows you, your network is truly your net worth. We know this for a fact on the job-search front. Sure, your work absolutely needs to speak for itself—but it helps when other people speak for you, too.

Do you feel trepidation about tapping into your personal network? Consider this staggering statistic: research has shown that networking accounts for up to 80 percent of all jobs landed at the executive level. The same holds true for consulting. All things being equal, people are simply more likely to hire someone they know or who has been recommended. So what does that mean for you? Get out there and start connecting. Who knows? Your next job or project or promotion could come from your next door neighbor (be it cubicle or cul-de-sac). Just ask Buyology's chief marketing officer Melissa Hobley, who learned to be fearless about making the right connections early on in her career: "Before I graduated, [during] my senior year of college, I wanted to work in government. I sent a letter to every single alum of my college [who] was an elected official, including congressmen, senators and mayors. I heard back from every person, and the meetings that I had led to four job offers."

Most would point to a Pink Slip Party, MeetUp group or alumni event as a great place to start, but Peter Shankman, founder of HARO, believes that there's no need to wait for special events to make the connections, saying that "everyone you meet is your networking event." Davidson Goldin, former editorial director of MSNBC, adds, "Everyone you've encountered you'll encounter again at some point, however unlikely that may seem. That doesn't mean you have to like everyone or even get along with everyone—that's impossible, and boring. But once you realize that the world gets smaller as you get older, you are more likely to give the people you work with or around the attention they deserve."

Keep an open mind, expand your circle as wide as you possibly can, and be sure to maximize all opportunities. One time, Jessica's boss asked her to meet with a woman who had just lost her job in corporate communications at a competing publishing company. When the woman arrived, she immediately seemed uncomfortable, saying at least twice in the first five minutes that she had thought she was meeting with Jessica's superior and that, perhaps, she should just reschedule. The woman answered every question with curt, one-word answers, and was not very gracious at the end of the meeting. Had she acted more pleasant and interested during her informational interview, she could have gotten leads—and even possibly a future job at Hearst. Instead, the woman's strange behavior and guarded responses led to nothing more than a wasted opportunity.

Once you have those contacts, it's important to stay in touch on a regular basis. Laurel Touby, founder of mediabistro. com, concurs: "I believe in lightly keeping in touch with all your contacts when you need them the least because the worst [thing] you can ever do is make a desperate call asking for help. Nobody will want to see you or have lunch with you. Call people up regularly enough that they're never worried that it'll be a horrible bore [when you do call]. 'Networking' is about taking when you need something. I need to network because I need a job, need a sale, etc. What's the solution? Don't use that word. Use 'connect' instead—I want to learn, share, help them. Think about the other person in the equation. What do they get from you?"

Sound Bite

"Ask not what your country can
do for you; ask what you can
do for your country."
—John F. Kennedy

Relationships Are a Two-way Street

To that end, PR people strive to forge relationships with key media and other contacts—it's imperative to getting things done. For example, over the years, Meryl has cultivated this kind of kinship with a morning show producer. What started as a segment about guacamole has evolved into a give-and-take friendship that allows the producer to come to Meryl with questions and requests, and Meryl goes to this producer with ideas to get honest feedback on what will work and what won't fly. It's been beneficial for everyone.

If you take nothing else away from this chapter, know that the most important thing you can do is to build a rapport between yourself and those with whom you are looking to do business. While that might seem obvious, what it means is, don't just go to someone when you need something. Go with something to offer. HarperCollins senior vice president Lisa Sharkey lives by the motto "The more you put out into the universe to help others, the more you'll get back." Take a page from her (and JFK's) playbook and don't only ask what your business partner/boss/colleague/intern/customer can do for you, but find out what you can do for them. By garnering favor and positioning yourself as supportive and helpful to others, it's likely that they will mirror the sentiment. It may not happen right away, but your helpfulness could pay off down the road.

Position Yourself as a Resource

By virtue of what PR professionals do—relate to the public about a person, place, experience, etc.—they are automatically a resource for information. To steal a phrase from *Seinfeld*, we have to become the master of multiple domains.

We'll talk about this a little more in Chapter 5, but being known as a person who can offer answers, feedback, and guidance is what makes a good publicist great. Being up on what's happening with a client and/or industry is one of the most essential PR skills to adopt—whatever line of work you're in. This tends to be particularly useful when dealing with press. The media—producers and journalists alike—tend to like a one-stop shop for information. Hand it over in a nice little package, and you're most likely to get the story told the way you want it. For example, Meryl handled publicity for the Veuve Clicquot Polo Classic, an annual event that draws celebrities including Prince Harry, Nacho Figueras, and Madonna, among others. It would be pretty easy for a brand to get lost with that kind of star power, so to ensure that Veuve Clicquot got significant play as part of the news stories that ran around the globe, Meryl and her team pulled together a whole range of information—from video to press releases, images to experts on champagne and polo—and offered it to the various media.

By putting everything at the media's fingertips, they made it more likely that the coverage would run and the brand would be included. Translate this from PR to the real world by doing as much legwork as possible and making the jobs of the people you're working with easier. That's how you get your call returned, the project done, the deal closed, the client you want, and the end result you were seeking.

Being in the Right Place at the Right Time Doesn't Work Unless You Know the Right People

We've always said if we could have one super power, it wouldn't be x-ray vision, super-human strength, or lightning speed. It would be perfect timing. But in our field, that kismet wouldn't mean much if we didn't have the right connections to leverage once we were there. That's a sentiment echoed by Beth Thomas Cohen, president/partner of B'squared Public Relations, who believes that "the combination of who you know, paired with your skills and experience, helps move you forward in the industry."

Stylist and author Phillip Bloch also credits the right people, place, and timing as his magic formula for getting ahead. "I never had a publicist other than myself—I just made the most out of the opportunities presented to me." He began in the 1980s as a model and then, at the suggestion of several editors, he began taking on stylist work. His entrée into the field came at a transitional time in Hollywood. According to Bloch, "It was like the Wild West out there. There was no one there to speak to the new Hollywood glamour and to connect with the younger starlets coming up—Sandy Bullock, Meg Ryan, Halle Berry, Jennifer Lopez, Salma Hayek. I helped forge the fashion connection between New York, Los Angeles, and Europe that is prevalent today. For me, it was being at the right place at the right time, and having the right attitude. I raised my hand, worked hard, and never batted an eyelash."

This combination apparently worked for Melissa Hobley, too, helping her land a new job: "I read a very interesting book on marketing by arguably the world's leading expert on branding, and I was riveted. I contacted the author, arranged a meeting because I knew that he could help a high-profile celebrity client of mine, and I developed a lot of interest in his work.

After the meeting, I followed up with a bold and fearless personal note saying that I wanted to be part of the company he was building and telling him that he needed me on his team. I also listed a few skills of mine that I knew he would need and, long story short, within a year, I had a job as his right hand."

 **Key Message:
Mobilize your forces**

Christine Kaculis, whose PR experience has ranged from boutique agencies to in-house brand management, says that you can't underestimate the ability to "mobilize your forces"—or get your personal advocates and support together—at a moment's notice. Most recently, she needed to do just that when making the shift from her vice-president position at an agency to an in-house one. "I heard about the position through word of mouth and got really excited–it was my dream job. I made sure that my key industry contacts knew, just in case they were needed for references or support."

Pay Attention to Your Surroundings

Being aware of the people around you can help you make friends—and avoid making enemies. The world is a lot smaller than it can seem and just as you are connected to lots of others, so are the people sitting next to you on the bus, standing behind you on the elevator, and dining at the next table. As a result, you need to be careful what you say, where you say it, and to whom you say it. Think about how much you unwittingly learn when you overhear people yapping loudly on their cell phones in public places (how annoying is that?). We'll talk about two rules we like to live by.

#1: The two-block rule

While this is not a PR-specific rule, per se, it's an important credo to which we hold fast, thanks to both personal experience. Despite an inevitable eagerness to debrief after walking out of meetings, a movie, show, or dining experience, it is standard practice to allow a two-block radius before launching into what went well or what didn't. This applies to walking into a meeting as well. You really never know who is in that elevator with you or walking behind you.

For example, on the way into a new business meeting for a travel company, a couple of our colleagues were strategizing about how to position work with a competitor, and who would take what piece of the presentation. When the elevator opened on the appropriate floor, the team stepped out, as did two others. As it turned out, those two happened to be in the meeting with them. What could have been disastrous was merely just embarrassing and anxiety-producing, as the team struggled to remember specifically what had been said.

There are even stories about companies who provided transportation for those who have just participated in a new business pitch or interview—only to tape the interaction inside the car or have the driver listening to the conversation. The two-block rule is just a good business practice; it comes in handy even when leaving a party or theater experience. Imagine the awkward moment you would experience if, after a Broadway show, you were walking down the street bashing the performance or the production—and the producer or the actress' mother was also leaving the theater and happened to be right behind you. Keep it zipped, and keep walking until you know that prying eyes and eavesdropping ears are out of range.

#2: You never know who is sitting next to you

Similar to the two-block rule, you should always beware of what you say in a public place, as you never know who is sitting right next to you and who that person may know. While we both have always adhered to the rule, the need for it became even more apparent when Meryl had dinner one night at a new restaurant in New York city.

"I was seated with my husband in a banquette. For a while, we were on our own; little by little the crowd filled in and, frankly, many were having loud conversations. To my left, a journalist from a trade publication was gossiping about the chef and his recent exploits. As it turns out, I had pitched—but had never met—that loquacious writer. From the conversations, I gleaned information about the publication's soon-to-be-released issues, challenging relationships with other chefs, and insider details about upcoming restaurant openings. To my right sat two journalists I had met once before—both friends with principals at my agency. Needless to say, I was thankful that I was aware of my surroundings and was able to adapt my conversation accordingly. The moral of the story: Keep the complaining or gossip to a minimum when in public; the person sitting next to you—or serving you your cocktail for that matter—might know someone who knows someone who could do something with the information you are sharing."

Sound Bite

"Be open to continuous learning. It facilitates networking and is a good reminder that there's always more to learn/someone to talk to."
—Linda Descano, Women & Co.

Key message:
Get schooled in networking skills

Though networking is an important part of career development, it is a skill set typically not taught in school or as part of job-training programs. It often requires you to step out of your comfort zone to go to places that are unfamiliar, connect with new people, and/or reconnect with old acquaintances and colleagues. Dana Fields Muldrow, senior manager of public relations at a large professional services firm, offers a few tips to help you develop this important skill:

- **Do your homework.** Before going to a meeting, event, or party, research the agenda/program and know who will be in the room. In addition, find out exactly where you are going so that you are not conspicuously late (or too early for that matter).
- **Prep what to talk about.** Once you've done your homework, prepare a few talking points, which should cover a variety of topics, including current events, breaking news, profession-specific items, movies, and personal information, among other things. They should be easy to remember and be relevant to the people that you will be meeting. If used properly, they will make you less anxious about networking, and will help eliminate the awkward silences that can occur.
- **Get comfortable.** Like most things, good networking requires practice! Attend professional events and programs, go to functions that your company sponsors, and attend parties where you might meet new people. The more you practice networking, the more comfortable you will be.

Talk to Me (and to Him...and to Her)

One of the key tenets of PR: Have the gift of gab. Being able to make conversation in any situation is an essential skill. And, as mentioned, it's important to gather as much information as possible before walking into a meeting or interview.

We do this with media all the time. Sometimes the most effective tool in figuring out the best pitch is to pick up the phone and float an idea by a contact. Media people love to offer their perspective and, if the story isn't right for them, they will often pass you along to one of their colleagues. (Just don't call them on deadline!) This can easily be translated when looking for a job or simply for more information about a company or industry in which you're interested. The so-called informational interview—coined by *What Color Is Your Parachute?* author Richard Bolles in his original book—continues to be a valuable tool in getting a job, getting connected, or getting a client. Meetings done for informational purposes—to learn more about an industry or company, typically—helps the interviewer glean tidbits to utilize in proposals or searches.

For example, after a few years in PR, Jessica briefly considered switching to full-time magazine writing. She had been freelancing for a few years on the side and was at a career crossroads, so she sent letters (There was no e-mail in those days!) to several people in the magazine industry—some of whom she knew, many of whom she did not—and got a lot of positive response. A number of them—from writers to managing editors, even to busy editors-in-chief—were willing to meet with her to talk about how they got to where they are, and to offer up their words of wisdom. Most of them told her that she'd have to start from the bottom of the editing rung, and that if she was able to freelance write while doing PR—a job she really enjoyed—she should continue on that road.

We love the story of Carrie Horn, a PR/marketing professional, who is well-versed in the benefits of the informational interview. In fact, she's used the tactic to successfully secure three separate positions throughout her career, speaking with upward of 100 people each time! An added degree of difficulty, each time she shifted jobs, she relocated as well. Her perspective: Most people see the effort of informational interviews as impressive—taking the time to get to know people takes guts and confidence. Companies appreciate those attributes in possible candidates. Other tips include:

- **Don't be shy.** Ask the people you're interviewing with for additional names of friends or colleagues whom they think would be a good resource.
- **Ask for feedback.** While meeting with people or after the fact, ask them to look over your resume and suggest changes that would make you a more attractive candidate.

- **Follow their lead.** Allow the informational interviewee to drive the discussion regarding what they would share with you.
- **Do your research.** It's important to know who you are talking to for each informational interview; find out their background and current responsibilities.
- **Take note.** Take notes during the meeting (you may want to ask first if it's okay) and then send a handwritten thank-you note to each person with whom you speak.

Marketing professional and networking champion Sheryl Victor Levy adds a couple more tips from her personal arsenal:

- **Keep it short and sweet.** If you're going to network with someone and you send them an e-mail, keep it short. Ask for 15 minutes only and be sure to use the word "brief."
- **Easy does it.** Make it convenient for your contact, and he or she will be more likely to help. Offer to go to his or her office and select a time that works within that person's schedule.

And, once you do call, e-mail with, or—even better—meet people who can help provide you with insight and information that will help you, here are some sample questions you may want to ask:

- How did you get into this business?
- What did you study in college or grad school? Do you think it helped you with your current career?
- What's your advice on the best way to break into this business/company?
- What do you love best about your job? Least?
- How important are personal connections in landing a job here?
- Did you always know you wanted to work in this field?

- What qualities do you look for in a great hire?
- What are the steps I need to take in order to move up the ranks?
- If there are no full-time positions available here, are there any opportunities for part-time, project, or freelance work?
- Is there anyone else you'd recommend I speak with?
- What do you wish you had known when first starting out in the business?
- Where do you see the industry going in the next five years?

**One-on-One Interview:
Carrie Horn—promotions director,
KALC/105.9 in Colorado; KQMT in Denver**

Q: **How did you get started with your impressive informational interviews campaigns?**

A: My first time, I was a senior in college. I began by accessing the Ithaca College database—my alma mater—and began putting out e-mails to alumni. I started with five people—alumni or students of current professors and went into the conversations without any specific expectations. I had a remarkably high success rate; alumni had a favorable experience at the college, so they were eager to "pay it forward" by helping me. Often, the people that I met with weren't actively looking to fill a position. Once they met me and I demonstrated my skill set, each place created a job for me. If that's not one of the strongest arguments for doing informational interviews, I don't know what is!

Q: **Did you ever get discouraged if the response was different than you expected?**

A: Sure, it can be frustrating or disappointing, but I considered every time someone e-mailed me back, or sent me a job posting, or referred me to another person as a little victory/success. It helped me keep focused on the greater goal.

Q: Aside from the actual positions, what did you get out of all of your informational interviews?

A: Confidence—I saw it as a possibility to gain awareness of my skill set; people are naturally inclined to give you feedback as part of this process.

Q: Did you ever feel uncomfortable asking for help?

A: Actually, what's important to remember is that everyone is interconnected and knows what it's like to look for a job and get in front of people. For the most part, they're willing to take the time to speak or meet with you. Ultimately, if they're smart, they'll understand that they could be asking you for thesame favor six years down the road!

Rude Awakening

The flip side of the "Don't you know who I am?" scenario is the equally irritating image of a snotty PR girl or guy, staffing the door of the "it" club or party and wielding a clipboard and its coveted guest list with an inordinate amount of power. Despite the pervasive Hollywood portrayal of a publicist as a dismissive flack directing people to stay outside the velvet ropes, in PR, rudeness is a one-way ticket out the door, never to return. In fact, according to daytime TV show producer Shant Petrossian, if a guest is rude to anyone—from the receptionist to the hair/makeup folks or the talent—he or she will most certainly not be invited back. If every interaction with every person is an opportunity, why blow it by being rude or disrespectful?

☑ **Fact Check**

According to a national survey done by Rasmussen Reports in late 2009, rudeness is on the rise in the United States. Seventy-five percent of adults say Americans are becoming ruder and less civilized.

We prefer to adhere to the "Nice Girl (or Guy) PR" philosophy: firm, but friendly, trumps disdainful and disrespectful anytime. And, because rudeness is apparently on the rise, being nice just might be your differentiating factor. We also apply the "everyone's important" rule when dealing with the media: just because someone might be blogging from his dorm room doesn't mean you should dismiss him when he reaches out to work with you. Jessica always tells her staff to treat all press equally (and nicely!)—whether they're from a small blog or a major media outlet—because you never know where someone's going to end up. Case in point: Brian Stelter started the blog TVNewser in college and he's now a successful television reporter for the *New York Times*.

According to public affairs pro Alexander Samuelson, "Manners count. Introduce yourself. Look [someone] in the face. The first step to networking is manners and social grace. When you're trying to meet a business executive at a function or trade show, it's assertiveness, manners, and knowing what you're going to say to them. They don't want to just B.S. with you. If there's one word to describe them, it's busy. They're incredibly busy. You have to have a reason to network." Digital marketing consultant Sheryl Victor Levy also reminds us to be just as nice to the assistants as to any executive. "They're the gateway, and they'll tell the senior people who they like. When you go on interviews, it starts with the receptionist. When you need a favor, the assistants, the mailroom guys, [those are the people who] can help you." How you treat them speaks volumes about who you are. In fact, Meryl learned early on from a mentor that the best PR comes from remembering people's birthdays and, when December rolls around, spreading a little holiday cheer; giving a small, festive token goes a long way to helping the unsung heroes of the office feel appreciated.

 Key Message:
Don't dismiss the maître d'

The importance of building your network is echoed by PR maven Heidi Krupp, founder and chief executive officer of New York-based

PR firm Krupp Kommunications. According to Krupp, "Anyone you meet, whether it's an assistant or a maître d', you never know if they're going to be a CEO someday. It's so important to meet people, make connections, and save them. Whenever I meet someone, I get [his or her] business card, write notes on the back about how I met [him or her] and what I can work with [him or her] on. Be out there. Most of all, you want to connect other people to each other. The more abundant you are with your network, the bigger your network becomes."

Key Message: Virtual is not a substitute for reality

It's not enough to have a virtual network of "friends" on LinkedIn or Facebook because it's still a distant and somewhat impersonal connection. According to book industry bigwig Lisa Sharkey, "People who are introverted can hide behind social media if in-person contact is too much for them." But it's important to get to know people face-to-face. Ask to meet with someone who works in a different department at your company or, if you're looking for work, clients, or investors, attend industry events and join professional organizations where you're bound to meet folks who might help you. Be outgoing, bring business cards, and vow to meet at least three new people before the event is over (or if at your own shop, in the next two weeks). Collect other people's contact information, and follow up with a call or note to schedule a time to take them out for coffee or lunch. The more acquaintances you have, the more they can connect you to others and widen your social and professional circle.

Get out!

The best way to connect with other people is to get out there, versus sitting in your house every night waiting for the phone to ring. It's not always easy to attend a business event or cocktail party where you don't know a soul and have to introduce yourself to perfect strangers. We're in the business of relating to the public, and it's even challenging for us sometimes!

But personal contact is exceedingly important when you're trying to raise your profile. It's one thing to hide behind e-mail, the phone, or social media, where you can "meet" people, but in a less personal way—think about how surprised you often are when you finally see someone in the flesh with whom you've been dealing remotely for ages. Jessica recalls one time at the start of her PR career when she asked an entertainment show producer whom she worked with often to go out for breakfast. When they finally met, they were both a bit stunned to discover that there was about a 30-year age difference between them—from their phone conversations, neither one could tell. It didn't matter, of course, and they forged a terrific relationship that lasted for years to come. Meeting in person absolutely helped strengthen that bond, as it often does.

 One-on-One Interview: Shawn Sachs, CEO, Sunshine, Sachs & Associates

We asked Shawn Sachs, founder of networking event Newsmakers, an after-work get-together designed to connect folks from the PR and media worlds, to tell us a bit about how this event started:

Q: How did the idea for Newsmakers come about?

A: There are obviously a lot of different kinds of networking opportunities out there. Each has its own DNA and process to how you network, and none of them is right or wrong. Our way is a little bit more laid back than most. It started when friend of mine, George Uribe, said, we should do these events and get people together." We knew a lot of people who had spaces and very quickly found people to give us a space at no charge with free drinks. We send out an e-mail. People come; they bring friends. The general thought pattern with us is that we don't do nametags, don't have a formal program. The idea is that you don't have to do anything. You want to come and hang out, great. You want to come and meet people, great. If all that happens is you reconnect with people you already know, great. In this day and age, you meet people in a digital way, but it's still not a handshake, it's still not a beer. If you do those things in concert, you build a relationship. We do it when we feel like doing it and a space becomes available. It has that no-forced way about it. It's great for me personally: I was managing more, pitching less, and still wanted to stay in contact and stay on people's radar.

Q: How did you launch it?

A: The publicists that I know came to me and ask, "Can you do this at our space?" As it grew, we were able to get better spaces and get three hours of free drinks and food. We do it in places all over the city and it's never the same look. That adds an element of fun and it doesn't get stale. It's easy to get people to come when you launch a new space. It just works. It's great for our company as well. I know that in our office there have been business and bookings born out of [Newsmakers]. It's part of our brand in a way—it was never an official thing, but it speaks "us." The openness—the fact that anyone can invite anyone else—makes it non-competitive.

Q: How has it grown?

A: We have people on our e-mail list and have a Facebook page. It grew so fast that it almost became too big. So we decided to add a charity component to it. We asked people for $20 that goes directly to a charity—from small and personal things to bigger organizations—which enabled us to get a handle on numbers and weed some people out.

Q: In addition to attending events like Newsmakers, what other things can people do to network?

A: Nobody likes to feels cornered. The air of desperation forces things in non-true patterns. Don't be so "you're on" or "you're off." Ken [Sunshine, founder of Sunshine, Sachs] stays engaged with people, and will give someone's son advice Stay in the mix, and sooner or later, something will happen. It takes years. I'm a big fan of being who you are. When you are, people are comfortable with it and believe it. [With Newsmakers], you look around the room and see the randomness of the people. It's very much who we are [as an agency]. If you build anything—in this case a networking event—it has to be what you are. If you try and force something, it feels weird.

What's in a name…and other important ways to connect with the right people in the right way

What's in a name? Everything.

In PR, we meet lots and lots of people every day. Meryl, admittedly, isn't great with names. As motivational speaker and author Dale Carnegie pointed out all those years ago, "There's nothing sweeter to a person than the sound of one's own name." To stave off panic in event situations, Meryl takes notes on the back of business cards as a way to keep track of everyone she meets in a night. She tries to follow up with an e-mail the next morning, to reinforce the connection. At meetings, she quickly jots names down as people introduce themselves, or lays out the business cards in front of her, mimicking how people are sitting in the room.

Alicia Ybarbo, *Today* Show producer and coauthor of *Today's Moms: Essentials for Surviving Baby's First Year*, offers this trick for recalling those you meet: "Make—and keep—contacts. If you have to write notes next to their name on your digital Rolodex, do it. Anything to help you remember those who help you is key."

But, what if you already know the people—or should know the people, you find yourself face-to-face with? Meryl employs a trick learned from the principal of her former agency. Instead of having to make a possibly disastrous slip, she greets people with "Nice to see you" in place of "Nice to meet you." It makes people feel acknowledged and avoids unnecessary backpedaling in most scenarios.

Have two to three "ice breaker" questions to keep the conversation going

We're sure you've been there: an awkward dinner party, elevator ride, or pre-meeting moment where the silence between you and another weighs down the air in the room. Some people are naturally better than others at small talk, but everyone should know how to diffuse an awkward or uncomfortable situation. We recommend having a few innocuous questions in your back pocket for such occasions. If you know about someone's family, it can be a great way to engage them by asking in general—"How old are your kids again?" Did they just take a vacation? That's also good fodder for cocktail chatter. "I hear you just went to Galapagos. I've always wanted to go there. What did you think about it?"

Financial services PR pro Dana Fields Muldrow always prepares talking points that cover a variety of topics, explaining, "Before I go anywhere, I always scan the newspapers (local and national), and I pay particular attention to the sports section. Whenever I end up in a conversation with a group of guys, it inevitably turns to sports. So rather than have nothing to say, I always have a factoid about the sport in season at the time. If you live in a major city where particular rivalries prevail (such as Yankees vs. Mets, Raiders vs. 49ers), try to know some of the players and their contributions to the teams."

Of course, there's always the tried and true fallback of the latest pop culture or current events, with one caveat: Stay away from controversial or political topics, please! Be it "Bieber Fever" or the latest blockbuster, come prepared with your perspective and ready to dish. Remember your key messages and what your end game is, and you should be good to go!

Smile and the world smiles with you

We know them—the people who light up a room. They're friendly. They're positive. They smile easily. These are people that others want to be around. Of course, you know those who are the polar opposite, whose dour and standoffish attitudes poison a space the moment they are in the vicinity. Wouldn't you rather be "walking sunshine" than "Badluck Schleprock," the Hanna-Barbera cartoon character from the 1970s who had a storm cloud literally hanging over his head at all times?

Media trainer and LXTV anchor Jane Hanson believes that the smile is the most effective means of communication we have. "It will help in tense situations. It speaks every language on earth. It's an instant way of making someone feel good. It's welcoming. It's magical." In fact, a smile can be quite disarming and contagious. A great example: One People magazine reporter we know takes this to heart. As part of her job, she conducts interviews on the red carpet at many high-profile events and, typically, that includes interviewing the attending celebrities. Whether the question she has to ask is good ("Who are you wearing tonight?"), bad ("How are you feeling now that you're out of rehab?"), or just plain awkward ("So what do you think of the most recent Mel Gibson meltdown?"), she always does it with a welcoming, friendly, non-threatening smile and encouraging nod. We know the trick and have even found ourselves cracking smiles as we watch her do her thing.

Expand your circle, strengthen your connections

A great way to get more involved in your industry and meet other folks with similar backgrounds or interests is to research professional organizations in your field, which offer great programs, educational opportunities, and networking events. There are also cross-industry networking groups such as your local Rotary Club, your college alumni associations, and national organizations such as Step Up Women's Network, which offer workshops, meet-ups, and conferences all over the country. Just as single people go to mixers and speed dating events, you can also look for opportunities to meet other people who may be helpful contacts at parties and events that are more casual than a buttoned-up trade show or conference. There are also numerous conferences and career-building events that take place across the country that can help you learn more about your industry, meet new people, and cultivate business leads or job opportunities. For example, Women for Hire (*www.womenforhire.com*), a terrific organization started by *Good Morning America*'s career expert Tory Johnson, offers career expos in various major cities. There are conferences and job fairs for every industry, so do a little research to find one near you.

◆ ◆ ◆ ◆

Your Personal PR Action Plan

1. Create talking points for three different types of situations (for example, cocktail party with the client; status meeting with your boss; face-to-face

with your direct report). Consider the audience and current events. Come up with four to five key messages to incorporate.

2. **Keep a week-long journal about your interactions with people.** Track your behavior (Did you say hello to people in the hallway? Were you patient with your intern? Did you chit-chat with the mail guy?) to make sure that you're being your own best publicist in every interaction.

3. **Consider a specific business contact and pretend that you are slated to have a work dinner with him/her.** Based on your knowledge and research about the person, craft three to five ice-breaker questions to help guide the conversation.

4. **Make a list of 20 people in your "network"— from those with whom you've worked or attended school, to neighbors or friends of friends.** Reach out to three to five just to say hello and check in on what's happening with them.

Chapter 5
The Message Is the Medium

"Regardless of how you feel inside, always try to look like a winner. Even if you are behind, a sustained look of control and confidence can give you a mental edge that results in victory."
—Arthur Ashe

In 2006, pop star Britney Spears did a sit-down interview with Matt Lauer on NBC's *Dateline*—with a wad of chewing gum in her mouth. Later that year, former New York District Attorney Jeanine Pirro was announcing her decision to run against Hillary Clinton for a Senate seat, and she paused for an interminable 32 seconds while attempting to locate a missing page of her remarks. In 2005, Tom Cruise had an excruciating interview—also with Matt Lauer (That poor guy gets all the doozies!)—on the *TODAY Show* where he called Lauer "glib," and criticized Brooke Shields for using psychiatric drugs to cure her postpartum depression. In early 2009, Joaquin Phoenix gave America one of the most awkward TV moments in history, where he famously appeared on the *Late Show with David Letterman* looking disheveled in sunglasses and a scraggly beard, and proceeded to give a near catatonic interview—while also chewing gum. (General rule of thumb, people: Take the gum out of your mouth before an interview.)

Believe it or not, celebrities and politicians can't be perfect all the time, but the instances previously mentioned demonstrate that a little advance prepping, coaching, common sense, and ability to think on your feet can never hurt when it comes to public speaking. Britney's handlers should have told her to ditch the Bubble Yum before the camera went on. It made her look not at all serious (and frankly stupid) while she was addressing topics like her marriage and motherhood. Pirro should have found a way to make a light joke or fill the space when she lost her place in the speech; standing at a podium in silence is awkward for both the speaker and the audience. Cruise, whose strong belief in Scientology is well-known, should have saved his thoughts on psychotherapy and medication for another forum, not one in which he was supposed to be promoting his next film. His righteous attitude and stubborn demeanor during that morning show interview alienated many people (including his "friend" Brooke Shields, to whom he later apologized). And Phoenix—well, where do we start? While many suspected—rightly so, as it turns out—the whole thing was a hoax tied to his mockumentary, *I'm Still Here*, it was highly uncomfortable and unprofessional.

Have you ever watched one of the Sunday morning network news shows and listened to a politician skillfully steer the conversation with the host back to his or her agenda? Or seen a seasoned talk show guest rattle off funny stories to the audience that seemed to have been created on the spot? Or even listened to a rousing speech given by a CEO at a conference or to his employees? Chances are, if they managed to do these things successfully, they'd gone through rigorous professional media training prior to the interview (or in most politicians' cases, prior to ever running for office). So what exactly is media training?

Used for years by PR professionals to coach executives, authors, professional athletes, actors, editors, and politicians, it's an effective way to teach someone how to streamline his communication style when doing interviews in order to come across as confident, knowledgeable, and clear with his messages. While most people won't have the opportunity to be interviewed on television or in a newspaper article, these skills can come in very handy during job interviews, presentations, or other interactions where you need to have your messages, body language, and presence nailed down.

Most professional media trainers charge as much as $2,500–$7,500 for a half-day or day-long session. During that time, they work with clients on how to create key messages, how to speak clearly and with energy (avoiding *ums, uhs, you knows,* and the ubiquitous shaking leg syndrome that happens when people get nervous), how to smile and be confident, answer tough questions, and dress the part. In most cases, the trainer will videotape clients doing mock interviews and then make them watch it back to see how they come across. Uncomfortable? Sometimes, but really effective.

If you can afford to hire your own coach in the future, great. But most people reading this book probably don't have a few extra thousand dollars lying around, so, in this chapter, we're going to give you some tips from experienced media trainers and a crash course on some of the key techniques used by them.

Key Message: Do the math

According to on-air personality and media trainer Jane Hanson, repetition is essential when communicating your key points. She says, "If you want to be sure people are truly getting the message—do the math:

9 x 1 = 0: If you say nine different things once, nothing sticks.

3 x 3 = 1–2: Say three key messages three times, and likely, what you're communicating will be heard once, if not twice."

Know What You Want to Say

In our world, we wouldn't dream of picking up the phone or going into a media interview without preparing the key messages we want to communicate. The same philosophy applies before walking into a job interview, presentation, or pitch meeting: always know ahead of time what you want to get across. How do you determine what that is? Ask yourself:

- What do I want to convey to my audience?
- If I can only communicate three important messages, what would they be?
- How do I get to all of them in the time I have?

For example, if you're interviewing for a job as an account manager for an advertising agency, what might you want to express? Some ideas:

- That you're especially good at developing client relationships.
- That you're someone who can handle tight deadlines (often imposed when working on a new ad campaign or commercial).
- That you are a good communicator and can work well with "creatives" (who can be stubborn personalities—we should know, as both of our husbands work at ad agencies!).

Have concrete examples to back up each message. According to media trainer Bill McGowan, founder of Clarity Media, it's important to show *and* tell. "Don't just tell someone you're a creative problem-solver; give an example of something you did on a previous job that illustrates that quality. Come into the meeting armed with anecdotal material—stories that frame you in a desirable light and makes the interviewer think, 'I want him/her on my team.'"

"Don't Close Your Windows"
...and Other Ways to Ace an Interview

Don't close your windows.

Body language expert Patti Wood deems specific areas of the body "windows" to a person's personality: the eyes, mouth, neck, chest/heart, knees, toes, and palms. When feeling confident, these are open. When feeling stressed out or hiding information, there's a natural tendency to close those windows. Be cognizant of touching your eyes, crossing your arms across your chest or clenching your teeth—all signs of the windows closing.

Straighten up.

Slouching demonstrates disinterest. Sit up straight, like your mom taught you! "To be your best publicist, you must always be aware about how you're coming across to people via your body language," says Jane Hanson.

Watch your pace and your length.

When we're nervous, our speaking pace automatically quickens, and we tend to drone on and on. The faster you speak, the more anxious you sound, and the less selective you can be about what you say. And the longer you talk, the more likely you are to say something you regret.

Be expressive.

In our quest to get through an interview without any drastic mistakes, we can flatten out emotionally. Speaking in monotone and stiffening up is a one-way ticket to Nowheresville. McGowan says, "Try to identify and talk about those things that organically get you enthused and excited so you can naturally show some passion."

Stay grounded.

According to Janine Driver, author of the *New York Times* best-selling book *You Say More than You Think*, if you are sitting on a chair and you cross your ankles, or wrap one of your legs around the other, you may be perceived as nervous or holding something back. Instead, women should shift their legs or feet, put them together and to the side. Another option: Use this gender-neutral move—put your feet flat on the ground.

In the blink of an eye.

Driver adds, "When you are in a location with bright and hot lights, it is inevitable that your eye blinks will increase due to dryness. Unfortunately, this blinking blooper could be perceived as nervousness and/or deception. The fix: keep eye drops in your purse, briefcase, or glove compartment. Before walking into the room or before hitting the stage, put two drops in each eye. This way your eyes will be hydrated, and you'll be less likely to increase your eye blinks."

Speak clearly and carry a big stick
(okay, you don't really need the stick).

Did you ever have one of those moments where you know exactly what you want to say, but it comes out all wrong? We've all been there. Even though something might sound good in your head, it takes planning and practice to ensure that it will get delivered the way you intended. Write down your key messages and study them. Tape yourself answering potential questions or running through your presentation or speech. Then play it back over and over until you get it right. Here are some things to listen for:

- Did you sound confident or nervous?
- Did you speak slowly and clearly, or were your words a jumble, spoken too rapidly, or filled with pauses and stammers?
- Did you communicate what you wanted to?
- Was your tone and pace appropriate for your audience?
- Were you too longwinded, or did you speak in brief sound bites?

 Key Message:
Skip the $5 words

Jennifer Zweben, a national network morning show producer, tells us what qualities make the best television guests (or presenters):

"When I evaluate if someone is a good guest, first and foremost, I want to be able to clearly understand what they're saying right off the bat. Also, I want to be able to learn something from them. For instance, if we're covering a difficult legal story, if the lawyer is able to make sense and actually tell you the facts in plain language, then you've struck gold.

If I can't understand what the guest is saying, and I have to push to make sense of it…forget it. Then I know the TV viewer would be confused, too.

Using big words and words that the majority of people don't understand is not wise. The best guests are the ones that can break complicated stories into an understandable story. Before an interview, write out talking points and use that as a guideline, rather than long-winded paragraphs.

Lastly, be yourself and be real."

You'd be amazed at how common it is for people to have nervous tics when they speak publicly—everything from saying *um* and *like* to fill in natural pauses, to playing with one's hair, or blinking too much. These are all physical manifestations of the anxiety we feel when we have to get up in front of a room of people or go on television. (For those of you old enough to remember *The Brady Bunch*, there's an episode where Jan Brady goes on TV and completely freezes up when she sees the red light of the camera.) Anyone who tells you they don't get nervous at all before doing these things is lying. Even the most experienced and well-known actresses and newscasters get a tad fluttery before going live. And that's a good thing—the same adrenaline that makes you nervous can make you energetic and engaging to an audience. You just need to know how to harness it in the right way.

For example, a good trick is to practice a speech or interview in front of the mirror. Pay attention to your body language, facial expressions, and energy level. Here's some advice to help you gauge whether you're on the right track:

- **Are you smiling?** It doesn't have to be a fake, plastered grin, but you also shouldn't look stern and somber. Communications strategist Davidson Goldin says, "Smile and pause very briefly before speaking. It's that simple. The smile puts others at ease and shows you're a team-player; the pause gives people the chance to become comfortable with you before hearing you." TODAY *Show* producer Alicia Ybarbo also believes that a smile helps, adding: "If you stutter or skip a thought, fix it and move on. Don't stop the conversation, because nine times out of ten, you're the only one who realized you said or did something wrong."

- **Are you using your hands to illustrate points?** This is a good thing, as long as you don't use them too much or put them in front of your face. You want to come across as comfortable, not stiff—and using your hands can help make you seem more approachable.

- **Does your voice go up at the end of a sentence?** Sometimes when we're nervous, that happens.

Keep your voice upbeat, but steady. Don't speak in a monotone or in run-on sentences. Most importantly, just as they tell you in yoga class: Remember to breathe! Says TV producer Shant Petrossian, "The best tip I have is to take a deep breath before you start speaking. That helps calm the nerves a bit...and makes sure your voice has strength, confidence, and doesn't strain at the end of the sentence."

Stop. Look. And, Most Importantly, LISTEN.

One of the most important elements of PR is listening to what others have to say. While many perceive that it's the publicist spewing information or hawking some product, public relations is truly a two-way conversation. Listening allows room to learn, to adjust the approach, and ultimately relate in a deeper way with your target audience. Sure, we encouraged you to be a "know-it-all," but that shouldn't be at the expense of listening. Unfortunately, in the traditional sense of the term, know-it-alls like to hear themselves speak and proclaim their vast knowledge on anything and everything. Some are so desperate to show off their wisdom that they choose to speak rather than listen. This is a mistake.

Instead of dominating the conversation, take some time to really hear what the other person has to offer. Observe his body language, tone, and pace of speaking. Does he seem like he's in a rush? Preoccupied? Glazed over? Or does he seem engaged, interested, and chatty? Let him ask you questions and tell you about the job or project, and what he's looking for. Come prepared with questions of your own, but be sure not to ask ones that have already been answered. You don't want to be like those local morning show anchors who are so busy listening to the control room speak into their hidden earpiece that they ask their guest a question about something that the person literally just addressed.

Sometimes you're so eager to share what you know that you forget to slow down and breathe. Stay calm, speak clearly, and pepper your conversation with bits of knowledge. You don't have to recite an encyclopedia's worth of facts and information in order to impress someone. Needless to say, you do not want to come across as a stalker who is familiar with every single detail of this person's work environment. Rather, the goal is to look as though you've done your research, but not as if you studied for a final exam.

Consider Your Audience

Every audience is different—just ask any stand-up comedian. They can practice their routine as much as possible, but when they get in front of a crowd, they have to gauge the tenor of the room and make-up of the audience. Is it a small, intimate room or a big arena? Is it college kids or older couples? Is it your co-workers or complete strangers? Do they seem eager to laugh or anxious to heckle? Once the comedian gets a read on the crowd, he can tailor his jokes, pace, and interaction for that particular group. Those who can't adapt to their surroundings risk bombing—and that's not a good feeling.

According to media trainer Mary Mayotte, "The more you know about your audience—demographic information, attitudes, biases, how much do they know and what's in it for them—[the more you have] a real 'leg up' when making that all-important connection and being remembered, not to mention making your presentation more targeted, and more fun and interesting for both you to deliver, and for the receiver of the information to find relevant. I always go the extra distance in researching this." Linda Descano of Women & Co. believes that the same can be said for communicating with your team in the workplace. "One of the things I learned early on is that people will not adapt to your communication style. Having been born and raised in the Northeast, I had a very direct 'get it done' style; this didn't necessarily fly in the Texas-based company [where I worked]. My style was similar to my boss's and was effective with him. While my boss was happy, the style was counter-productive with my team. When my performance review came around, the HR person thankfully shared the feedback. I now spend a lot of time getting to know the audience—whether they are my co-workers or a conference room full of people."

When you're put in front of a new audience, you have to get a read on them right away. Say you're a freelancer who's doing a capabilities presentation to a potential client, for example. You want to come across as the right fit for their project or business, so during preparation, ask yourself:

- **What kind of company are you presenting to?** Is it a big corporation or a small business? An accounting firm or a marketing agency? An accounting firm might appreciate a more straightforward and fact-based presentation, whereas a hip marketing company might be open to some fun ideas presented in a creative and peppy way. Do some research on what clients and projects the company has worked on in the past. Get an idea of their capabilities, accomplishments, and style before going in.

- **What's their vibe?** Buttoned-up and professional? Creative and casual? Depending on the answer, you want to dress appropriately for the surroundings. Don't show up in a suit and tie if everyone there wears jeans and sneakers. You'll feel out of place and out of sync with everyone else in the room. What if you don't know ahead of time what the company's style is? Be resourceful: have lunch outside their building one afternoon and watch how employees are dressed. Or see if you can get in touch with someone who works there, or a person who knows one who does so you can gain some important intel before your interview or presentation.

• **How can your expertise meet their needs and how can you communicate that?** Chances are, you're competing with other people for the same business so you have one chance to demonstrate why you're the one they should choose. Have your key messages in mind and punctuate them throughout the presentation. You want people to leave the room impressed with what you have to offer.

Key Message:
It's not about you, it's about them

Joyce Newman, founder of The Newman Group, has been helping professionals improve their communications skills in a variety of speaking situations—from platform presentations to media interviews—since 1975. We asked her, "What's the most important thing to focus on when public speaking?"

"*The audience, the audience, the audience.* The more you can know about them, the better so that you're really speaking to them, leaving them with takeaways, and not force-feeding them with information. You can do a little survey, talk to the meeting planner and find out who the audience is, what they know about your topic, how much do they need to know and, most importantly, what's in it for them. If you figure out why they're coming to hear you and what the payoff is to them, and keep coming back to that, then you're going to have a listener. A good speaker will also anticipate the questions that could get asked and incorporate answers into the speech. Make it about the audience, and get out of your own head. Lose the 'I' word and put in 'you' instead—you being the audience. Everyone in that audience has an ego—figure out a way to connect with them. Learn how to put a thought across to a person with eye contact and let it sink in. Don't dart around like a bird on a stick.

Wait for a nod, and then move onto the next person."

Sound Bite

"According to most studies,
people's number-one fear is
public speaking. Number two is
death. This means to the average
person, if you go to a funeral,
you're better off in the
casket than doing the eulogy."
—Jerry Seinfeld

Connect to Communicate

Whether you're speaking in front of a crowd, in a business meeting, or at a job interview, it is essential to determine who will be listening to your viewpoint and how you can customize your information for their ears. When it comes to making speeches and presentations, one size does not fit all. Most experienced speakers and television guests—such as Bill Clinton, Tom Hanks, Oprah Winfrey, and Tony Robbins—enter a room with some sort of script in mind but, to the audience, it never sounds like one. That's because they always change it slightly depending on the audience and energy in the room. Having booked a lot of our clients' speaking engagements over the years, here are some simple tips we've picked up along the way:

- **Arrive early.** If you're speaking in front of people, take a page out of media trainer and on-air talent Jane Hanson's book. She typically arrives about 15 minutes before she's set to take the stage. She walks around, asks questions, and then interweaves the anecdotes into her remarks. Parsons The New School For Design professor Tom Handley adds, "Always arrive early to any meeting or event, so you can own the room. Be there to welcome people, even if it isn't your event."

- **Listen to others.** If you're on a docket to speak after others, take notes while they're talking and, if possible, refer back to something one of them said in their speech or presentation: "As Margaret mentioned earlier, there's no time like the present to start investing in the stock market."

- **Localize your speech.** If you're on a local morning show or speaking on a panel, use the host's or moderator's name or refer to the market you're in: "Thanks for having me, Rose. As anyone who's taken the NYC subway knows, germs are everywhere."

- **Radiate warmth.** We've been lucky enough to have been in a room, on separate occasions, with both President Clinton and Oprah, both of whom possess the gift of making each person in their presence feel as if he or she's the only one. Not everyone possesses their natural charisma, but if you act warm and approachable when addressing an audience—whether it's one person or 1,000—you'll come across as though you really care about what they think (and hopefully you do).

- **Make eye contact.** According to Bill McGowan, it goes back to what our mothers used to tell us: "Look me in the eye and say that." If you engage people with your eyes versus darting around the room or staring at your notes, they're more likely to pay attention and feel that you're speaking to them directly. People who are shifty-eyed somehow seem less trustworthy or confident, and can lose their audience very easily as a result.

- **Be short, sweet, and clear.** According to Davidson Goldin, the three most important things to focus on when speaking publicly are "clarity, brevity, and confidence." You want your audience to understand you, get a clear picture of what you're trying to communicate, and feel that you know what you're talking about.

- **Be genuine.** When booking guests, daytime TV producer Shant Petrossian says he looks for "someone who is honest, genuine, and has a sense of humor. I enjoy working with or producing those guests that are the same off-camera as they are on-camera."

- **Spice it up.** If appropriate, bring props or something fun to break the ice. We've been known to bring candy to a late afternoon meeting to get people's sugar levels up so they'll pay attention—a sweet little "bribe" rarely hurts!

 Sound Bite

"We have, as human beings, a storytelling problem. We're a bit too quick to come up with explanations for things we don't really have an explanation for."
—Malcolm Gladwell, *Blink: The Power of Thinking Without Thinking*

 News Flash: Communicate on all levels

So much of communication comes through not what we say, but our tone, body language, and delivery. In coaching our clients for interviews or public speaking, we always advise them to stay upbeat and try not to get their dander up, even if someone's line of questioning rattles them. When a person is tense, nervous, angry, defensive, or disingenuous, those feelings are often broadcast to other people in the room, even if that person doesn't know it. Take Tiger Woods' press conference in February 2010, apologizing for his adulterous behavior. While his words sounded sincere, his demeanor was anything but. There were a couple of moments where he seemed genuine, but overall, the golf star came across as stiff, disconnected, and clearly reading right from a script.

Janine Driver, body language expert and author of *You Say More than You Think*, likens body language to the FedEx logo: "Have you ever spotted the subliminal arrow in the FedEx logo? (It's between the bottom part of the "E" and the "x".) In 1994, Mr. Lindon, the Senior Design Director at Landor Associates in San Francisco created this award-winning logo, with the intent that it would be a symbol of both FedEx communicative attributes: speed and precision. The way you sit, stand, cross your arms, or move your feet, can break or build *your* brand. Yes, our body language reveals far more information then we might think and, much like the FedEx logo, these signals are subconsciously interpreted by others. Surprisingly, most people are totally oblivious to their own body language, so the discipline of controlling these gestures can be quite challenging."

The Takeaway: Ask yourself, "What do I want *my* subliminal message to be?"

Boy, That's a Tough Question

Sometimes all the planning in the world can't prepare you for a tough question or a change in topic during an interview. In order to get through unscathed, you need to know how to handle these situations. For starters, you don't have to answer every question thrown at you. There are plenty of ways to deflect questions that make you uncomfortable, or for which you don't have an answer. Some rules of thumb:

- **Go back to your key messages.** If an interviewer tries to get you off track or asks you something you'd prefer not to address, say, "That's a good question, Bob, but what I'd really like to talk about is X..." That way, you can return to your agenda without seeming rude. Remember, you are in control of your interview. You have a mission, and that's to communicate your wisdom and expertise on the topic you came to discuss. Political pros call this "message discipline": making sure that you stay "on message" makes it less likely that what you say will be taken out of context.

- **Be honest.** If you genuinely don't know the answer to something, don't make it up. Instead say, "To tell you the truth, that's not something I'm equipped to answer at this time. Can I get back to you with my thoughts?" or "I wouldn't want to give you an answer to something that's out of my realm of expertise."

- **Answer without really answering.** This is a classic PR trick. We don't believe in saying "No comment." It is not very creative, and makes you sound as if you're hiding something. There's always a way to respond cleverly to a question, even if you're not exactly giving the answer being sought. What if you're interviewing for a job in another part of your company, and the interviewer asks you what you don't like about your current department? You have to be careful here because you don't want to sound like you're badmouthing your current boss, particularly if you end up not getting the new position. And because it's at the same company where you already work, there's a risk that any negative comments might get back to your supervisor. So what do you say? We'd suggest something like, "I've learned a tremendous amount in my current position, and have been able to work on a number of interesting projects. What I'm looking for next is an opportunity to put my talents to use in a new way and expand my experience in X, Y, and Z [plug in whatever is relevant to the new job]." That way, you're not insulting anyone, but you're also answering the question in a way that reinforces what makes you a good candidate.

Sound Bite

"Before anything else,
preparation is
the key to success."
—Alexander Graham Bell

Spontaneity Takes a Lot of Practice

You know when an actress wins an Oscar and after arriving at the podium, says, "Oh my God, I didn't expect to win, so I didn't prepare anything," then proceeds to launch into an eloquent, witty speech? Well, the ruse is up. She *prepared* to say that she didn't prepare—all part of a preconceived plan to make her look modest and humble.

In the best-case scenario, you will present yourself in a public speaking situation or interview as comfortable, confident, and natural. But "winging it" rarely works. You have to study hard to come across that way. Imagine if, when you were 16 or 17, you thought you could take your driver's license test after playing *Pole Position* a few times. It may have seemed easy, but a simulated driving experience is not the same as actually getting in the car and practicing making U-turns and parallel parking. The latter, of course, would set you up much more effectively to pass the test with flying colors.

As someone who has booked hundreds of interviews in her career as a television producer, Alicia Ybarbo advises people to "prepare a few answers to the most commonly asked questions that you've already been asked. Practice them, but don't over-rehearse them so that you sound robotic. You want to keep a conversational tone about you. If you don't have a friend to bounce answers off of, practice in front of a mirror, your pet, or your Flip video. Not only will you be better versed on your own information, but you'll get a boost of self-confidence from the amount of preparation you've done."

Going back to someone we mentioned earlier in the chapter, if you've ever seen Tom Hanks appear on a late-night talk show, you'd know that he's a terrific guest. Even back in the 1980s when he was just a stand-up comedian starring in a little sitcom called *Bosom Buddies*, he was always engaging, entertaining and funny. He seemed to come up with spontaneous anecdotes to share on air but—trust us—those stories were all planned well in advance of his arrival. He probably even had a pre-interview with one of the producers before the show so that they could prepare the host to have his own "off-the-cuff" banter. Bottom line: Hanks is a pro. But the more you pay attention to people who are really good, the more you can learn and apply those lessons to yourself.

Key Message:
Train like an athlete

According to Davidson Goldin, founder of communications strategy firm Goldin Solutions, "Preparation makes a big difference. Just as athletes and performers train before the big game so their movements become second-nature, you need to be totally comfortable about what you're presenting and how you're presenting yourself in order for you to be relaxed, confident, and charming."

Your Personal PR Action Plan

1. **Build out your elevator pitch to be a short speech about yourself and what makes you special.** Focus on three key attributes or goals. Be sure to decide who your audience is. Are you interviewing for a job? Are you talking to your boss about a promotion? Are you pitching new business? Tailor your speaking points to that audience.

2. **Practice your speech in the mirror.** (It will feel silly but just pretend you're in one of those movie montages where the main character practices introducing himself in front of the mirror!) Do you seem comfortable, confident, and clear? How's your body language, eye contact, posture? If you were the listener, would you be convinced?

Chapter 6

Looks Aren't Everything (but They Sure Help)

"Style is the image of character."
—Edward Gibbon

How many Hollywood movies hinge on a simple wardrobe change as a transformative experience for the character? From *My Fair Lady* and *Mean Girls* to *The Devil Wears Prada*, pop culture points to the impact of appearance. Public relations is an image business, plain and simple, and how you look is as much your calling card as the one in your wallet. But, you don't necessarily need to be the best-looking or best-dressed; you just need to make a statement.

Whether you're a man or woman, everything about your appearance—your haircut to your shoe choice—speaks volumes about who you are and where you're going, whether you are consciously trying to communicate that or not. Don't worry—you don't have to run out and purchase the latest and greatest accessory, or spend a ton of cash to overhaul your wardrobe. This chapter will walk you through tips and tricks of the trade from some of the top stylists in the business and ideas about creating your style and leveraging looks to get noticed.

Key Message: Everything counts

According to stylist and Purple Lab Creatrix Karen Robinovitz, image truly *is* everything: "From your business card to your letter-head to the way you present yourself and your collateral—every ounce leaves an impression, so make it a good one."

Back to Basics

According to stylist and former fashion publicist Jonny Lichtenstein, who has worked with such high-profile designers as Helmut Lang and Tory Burch, "The safest way to dress and impress is to stick with chic, simple, understated clothing. Men should invest in a gray or black, light wool, two-button suit. For women, keep color, accessories, and skin to a minimum. Basic shapes such as a wrap dress or a tie-neck blouse paired with a pencil skirt are sure to impress." Stylist Erin Busbee concurs, "A safe and professional way to dress for your business meeting is in a black suit. It doesn't have to be an exact match—there is no reason why you can't buy a nice black blazer and wear it with a pair of wide-leg, chic pants that you already have in your closet. When in doubt, guys (if not on a job interview or in an über-formal setting) should wear dressy khaki pants (the kind you can still wear with dress shoes), a blue, crisp, button-down shirt and a good-looking tie. Bring a navy blazer. You can always ditch it at the last minute if no one else is sporting one."

Start with a solid foundation for your wardrobe first. Core essentials for women include:

- A flattering and fashionable black dress.
- Classic black suit.
- A bright, white button down shirt.
- Sophisticated, dark wash jeans (at least one pair).

- A basic black skirt (shape based on body type).
- Comfortable and chic black pumps.

Men should have the following:

- Classic navy, black, or charcoal gray suit.
- A fantastic tie (consider a twist on a classic stripe or dot pattern, created in a high-quality fabric; no novelty images or patterns).
- Khaki pants.
- A pair of dress shoes.
- At least one white button-down shirt (although you're likely going to need more).
- One blue button-down shirt.
- A short sleeve polo shirt.
- A pair of khaki shorts (knee length or just above).

Start by shopping your closet, as recommended in Phillip Bloch's smart and thrifty tome, *The Shopping Diet*. Don't have some of the basics above? Ultimately, if you *do* have to open your wallet, the key is to spend smartly. *Marie Claire* fashion director and *Project Runway* judge Nina Garcia believes in investing in a couple of amazing pieces each season—be it a basic you'll wear for years to come or a can't-live-without-it statement item such as a dramatic necklace or embellished jacket. You can then fill in the rest of your wardrobe with an affordable mix of trendy and classic items. Less-expensive items can always be elevated when worn with investment buys.

The good news: To borrow the phrase from the classic 1970s commercial for The Ritz Thrift Shop in New York, "You don't need a million to look like a million," particularly these days. There are tons of affordable choices ranging from online flash sale sites like Gilt Groupe and Rue La La to designer collaborations with big box retailers including Target, H&M, and Kohl's to pick up some of the basic building blocks of anyone's wardrobe. Stylist and entrepreneur Karen Robinovitz adds,

"Consignment shops are a great resource for designer handbags at a good price. I think a good handbag makes a powerful punch in the style department."

 Sound Bite

> "Know first who you are
> and then adorn yourself accordingly."
> —Epictetus

 Key Message:
Be yourself

According to Christine Kaculis, director of communications for Veuve Clicquot Champagne, it is highly important to cultivate a strong sense of self and personal style in PR, and in the workplace in general. "As a publicist, you are the expert. You know what's cool and makes people tick. Your boss or clients want to know that you have a unique point of view and stand by what you think. You should never be afraid to be you, and let it shine in everything you do. Never listen to a boss who tells you to suppress your style— media and clients respond to individuality."

Find your Signature Style

Diane von Furstenberg has the wrap dress. Donald Trump has his hairstyle. Lady Gaga, her crazy outfits. *Vogue* Editor-in-Chief Anna Wintour, her stick-straight bob and sunglasses. What all of these famous people have in common is a signature style that defines them and is readily recognizable. What's *your* signature style? Think about how you might create it, if you don't already have one. We're not suggesting you have to be as extreme as the aforementioned folks, but consider what would make you stand out from the crowd. A chic new hairstyle? Bold jewelry? A cool pair of vintage glasses? A pop of color added to an all-black wardrobe? A collection of cuff links to jazz up your standard navy suit?

How you look sends a strong message about your personality. According to Adam Glassman, creative director of O, *The Oprah Magazine*, "Find a style that makes you feel like a million bucks. That's your 'uniform.' You should be wearing some version of it every day."

Since Jessica has known her, Hearst's chief communications officer Debra Shriver has sported a signature cropped gray hairstyle that's chic, modern, and bold—just like Shriver. Not everyone could get away with that look, but on her it really works. Meryl's look, on the other hand, is "modern vintage" and her wardrobe mixes vintage shift dresses, blazers, and brooches with of-the-moment shoe styles and bags. Her rule of thumb is to incorporate at least one vintage item into each outfit. If she just purchased a new black dress, for example, she will layer on several vintage necklaces to add a bit of pizzazz. On a day she opts for that red chiffon dress from the 1970s, she'll throw on a black cardigan and simple patent pumps to tie in the look. Just remember to dress appropriately for your industry, body type, and age. Create a look, but don't make it a costume. You want to stand out for the right reason, not because you're a 60-year-old who wears miniskirts or blue eye shadow. According to Jonny Lichtenstein, "When creating a signature style, remember to stay true to yourself. If you are conservative, don't fall victim to fashion trends. Being classic and simple is a very strong signature style onto itself. If you are a fashionista, then be daring and experiment. In either case, what feels comfortable will eventually emerge and may lead you towards the kind of company you want to work for."

 Sound Bite

"Whether you're a man or
woman, a great haircut and pair
of shoes are a person's bookends.
Everything else you can improvise."
—Sarah Shirley, stylist

One-on-One Interview:
Sadah Saltzman,
Hair & Makeup Artist, Salon A.K.S.

Hair and makeup pro Saltzman, who works at one of New York City's top salons, shares her best tips for creating a look that's appropriate for you:

Q: How important is hair and makeup when you're trying to get noticed in a good way, and why?

A: Hair and makeup is very important because, let's face it, your appearance is what people look at first. It's what they judge you on. If you are well-put-together, you are going to come off as an organized and professional person. If you're a mess, then that's what people will assume you are. Even for men, the way your hair is styled has a lot to do with others' opinions about you. A shaggy beachy 'do' for a man gives off the impression of a laid back kind of guy—not so professional. But style it neatly combed on a part and you're ready for Wall Street. You may not always style yourself the way you do for a job interview, but there is a definite difference between professional and personal style. You always want to look clean and put together. You want your hair and makeup to look deliberate and not a mistake.

Q: How should people create a personal style or a look that reflects what they're trying to accomplish?

A: Make your personal style something that you can maintain and realistically pull off. With makeup, pick something that you would like to accentuate—lips, eyes, skin. Do not do all at once. Remember you want to feel confident; a job interview is not where you want to try out a new trend. Do the same with your hair. If you have really curly hair and you're not great at blow-drying it, don't make your personal style smooth and straight. Work with your curls/wear your hair in a way that's going to look its best.

Q: What should you think about when you're trying to determine what look you want to achieve?

A: Consider the message you're trying to send.More polished and refined? Or wild and sexy? Know that what you look like is what people first judge/assume about you. A bold lip can be fun and playful if worn with loose wavy hair, but then can look professional and classic when worn with hair pulled up.

Q: Are there certain rules/faux pas that should be considered when doing hair and makeup for different settings (i.e. interview with a bank vs. a fashion designer, public speaking opportunity, TV appearance)?

A: Of course there are certain rules. You need to look appropriate for each setting. If you're going into the office, or on an interview with a bank, you want to look clean, crisp, and ready. Hair should look polished and makeup clean. If you're wearing your hair down, it should be finished looking and makeup should be subtle. When you're sitting in an interview, you want them to be paying attention to what you are saying and not to the makeup on your face. If you're in the fashion industry, you can play around with your look a little more. However, I recommend not experimenting with trends until you get the job. So, on an interview, I would still keep it sleek.

If you're speaking in public, think about how far away you are from the audience. You want to be seen. You want your eyes and your lips to speak to your audience. Make sure you really make those eyes stand out. Even a little more eyeliner than you would normally use can make a difference. Take what you would do and turn it up a little bit. Make sure your hair is styled in a way that you won't be fidgeting with it while you're speaking.

Dress to Impress (Not to Blind) Your Audience

You want to dress for the occasion and the audience. If you look at what TV show hosts and anchors wear on air, they usually stick to solid colors, simple necklines, tailored looks, and minimal jewelry. While there are special considerations for television with the lights, audio, and cameras to worry about, most of these rules apply to interviews and presentations as well. Network morning show producer Alicia Ybarbo advises: "When it comes to wardrobe, simple is best. This is not the time to try a new look. At the same time, you want this audience to remember you, so try to think of *one item* that sets you apart from the crowd. A fun colored blouse, a great bracelet, or a wild pair of shoes will compliment your look." Or, for men, perhaps a pocket square or a jewel-toned tie.

On the other hand, here's what's best to avoid wearing when on camera or in front of an audience:

- **Busy patterns.** You can wear patterns, but stay away from those that might be too distracting to the eye.
- **Big jewelry that sparkles or clanks.** Especially on TV or at a podium, these can reflect off the lights or get picked up by the microphone.
- **Stained or ripped clothing.** This seems like a no-brainer, but before you leave the house, check for stains, snags, and pulls. You want to look neat, not unkempt and unprofessional.
- **Anything too revealing.** Keep your necklines high and your hemlines low. No miniskirts, low-cut dresses or blouses, tank tops, or too-tight dresses. While this should be needless to say, we'll say it anyway: wear undergarments and make sure they fit well. Unlike our friend Britney Spears, you certainly don't want to get your audience's attention for the wrong reason.

- **Short-sleeved dress shirts and too-short ties.** This one's for the guys. Nothing will make you look more like a used car salesman than this ensemble. Of course, if you're interviewing for a job as a used car salesman, then don't let us stop you! But generally, men should wear a well-fitting, button-down shirt and, if the occasion calls for a necktie, the tip of it should hit your waist line, not your torso. Stay away from "crazy" ties with sports team logos, cartoon characters, or the like. Keep it classic and simple.

 Sound Bite

> "For great work style: assess
> the nature of your profession
> and look to your boss—
> and their boss—for clues to
> get-ahead style."
> —Adam Glassman, *O, The Oprah Magazine*

Life = Runway

One of our favorite features in the *New York Times* is "Life as a Runway" column, where photographers snap people as they stroll through the streets of New York City, tying them back to burgeoning trends in the fashion world. This voyeuristic layout lends even more credence to stylist Erin Busbee's perspective that people should always look their best—even when just heading out for a quick errand. She asks, "What if you come across an amazing networking opportunity, and you can't capitalize on it because you're [dressed inappropriately]? Or meet the person of your dreams, but you're in sweats?! Pull yourself together even for a quick stop at Wal-Mart." Laurel Touby, founder of mediabistro.com, agrees and encourages everyone to "be aware of your dress" even in casual settings, underscoring that no event or social occasion is a throwaway. If you "think of them as potential stepping stones to a job or a professional opportunity," it becomes vital to always pay very close attention to what you wear. "It's important to be aware of how you're coming across...I'll wear a brightly colored blouse or crazy shoes. I wear orange pumps, and it's a conversation piece."

	Key Message:
	Invest in what you love

Marie Claire's Nina Garcia recommends investing only in pieces you truly love: "When you look into your closet, you should like everything you see, from the basic items to trendier buys. When you put together looks that fit well and that you feel comfortable and beautiful wearing, that's a sure sign you've created your own signature style."

Don't Wear a Ballgown to a Ball Game

In our business, looking the part is key to being able to communicate effectively to your audience. In simple terms: Don't wear a ballgown to a ball game. But often, it isn't that easy. For example, while technically the agency's hospitality group, Meryl's team had become the catch-all for accounts that didn't quite fit into the more rigidly defined groups such as fashion, beauty, and design. As a result, they often had to switch gears from business to video games to spirits or luxury brands at the drop of a hat. Each client had a dress code or vibe that needed to be matched when meeting face-to-face.

According to Meryl, "It wasn't unusual for someone on my team to do three or four costume changes a day, à la Superman, moving from jeans and a casual t-shirt to a pencil skirt and pumps. Frankly, at first there was resistance—even resentment: What do you mean I can't wear this dress or those shoes?

Shouldn't I be able to express myself? The truth is that clothes do make the man (or woman). Appearances in general are important (look neat, professional, etc.) and the clothing one wears can, at a minimum, be a distraction and hindrance to understanding; at a maximum—a significant barrier to entry."

In fact, a candidate recently came in to interview for a job in Jessica's department wearing jeans. When the HR person told her she was underdressed for what was essentially a corporate position, the woman said, "Well, I had a cute dress picked out this morning but it was raining, so I wore this instead." Her foolish choice of wardrobe (and, frankly, foolish choice to tell human resources the real reason for her casual wear) was unfortunate because she had a very solid resume and would have been seriously considered for the position had she dressed more appropriately.

Whether you are trying to land a job working somewhere full-time or freelancing, you have to remember that companies will hire and promote people who help them put their best foot forward in every scenario. No matter what you're doing, you are, in essence, the face of the company.

To that point, we know of one company that takes this a step further: as part of the interview process, a candidate is asked to attend a cocktail event. The reasoning: In addition to understanding the way someone dresses for a formal, clearly defined professional meeting, the potential employer is able to assess how the person would choose to present him or herself at an after-work function. Is the dress too flashy or sexy? Is he sporting too casual a look for the situation? All other things being equal, the person who is able to navigate this issue effectively ends up with the position, plain and simple.

Crimes Against Shoe-manity
...and Other Fashion Faux Pas to Avoid

If you're on the right professional track, don't let yourself be derailed by a fashion faux pas. Some of today's top stylists weigh in on how to stay the course:

- **Crimes against shoe-manity.** Shoes should be polished and in good shape. According to stylist Dayna Spitz, men must own a good pair of lace-up shoes; women should have a good pair of heels that are stylish, but sophisticated. Jonny Lichtenstein recommends investing in a well-made shoe in both black and brown: "For men, a classic oxford or wingtip never goes out of style. For women, a stacked pump and a sling-back work flawlessly from season to season."

- **Not a fit.** Sarah Shirley laments, "I see so many people wearing things too tight or too big. Since [items] off the rack weren't made specifically for you, it stands to reason that they won't fit you perfectly. Take time to get them tailored to fit correctly."

- **Tight situations.** According to Lichtenstein, women usually make the mistake of not knowing what to do with their legs. The general rule is bare legs in the spring and summer, and if you are going to wear hose, tights, or stockings, make sure the shoe is closed in the front and the back.

- **Showing skin.** Hemlines should be either just right above or right below the knee. Women should avoid showing too much skin or cleavage. Erin Busbee adds, "Even when I'm going out with my husband on date night, I make sure I keep the skin exposure to one area. For example, if I'm wearing a short dress, I'll put a shrug or blazer over the dress to cover my arms and chest."

- **Too trendy.** According to Nina Garcia, trend overload in the workplace always looks wrong. "The office is no place to test-drive multiple competing fads, even if you work in a supremely creative environment. Classic, well-made pieces will never steer you wrong."

- **Wear what works for you.** Speaking of trends, we see it all the time: every season there's a style—be it the maxi dress, jeggings, or whatever—and, in an instant, every Tom, Dick, and Harriet is adopting the trend, regardless of whether it really works for them or not. Celebrity stylist Phillip Bloch encourages everyone to learn to "stay in your own lane in fashion." To put it another way, as Garcia says, "Just because it looks good on your best friend, co-worker, or celebrity style icon doesn't necessarily mean it will work for you! Dress for what fits your figure and your personality."
- **The casual casualty.** Dayna Spitz, who gives seminars at corporations on this topic, says, "Some of the biggest mistakes people make are dressing too casually to the office (flip flops, short shorts or mini-skirts, sundresses, etc.). Most inappropriate dressing happens during the summer months."
- **Label liability.** Just because you're trying to get ahead doesn't mean you suddenly need that flashy watch or designer bag. According to Lichtenstein, the more humble one appears guarantees more respect from their peers and employees.

Your Personal PR Action Plan

Create a style board

You don't have to spend a fortune to have your own style—look through magazines, watch movies, and pay attention to celebrities whose looks you admire.

1. **Write down five adjectives that describe your personality and five people whose style you like.**
2. **Next, jot down five to 10 items currently in your closet that you love and why;** your favorite color; best body asset (small waist, defined biceps, long

legs); and your lifestyle (casual, formal, professional, creative) and work environment (a graphic designer may need to dress differently than a banker).

3. **Decide on one key element that could be your signature** (for women: bold jewelry, high heels, belt-
ed dresses; a headband; for men: a pocket square,
preppy tie, cool sneakers, horn-rimmed glasses)
and try to incorporate it into your wardrobe for the
next week and see how it feels.

Chapter 7

What Do I Have to Do to Get Noticed Around Here?

"There is only one thing in the world worse than being talked about, and that is not being talked about."
—Oscar Wilde

In public relations, we attract the attention of the media and consumers with our message by slicing through the "clutter" that surrounds us everyday. For example, when Meryl pitches one of the chefs she represents to television shows, she's up against endless culinary experts—from other chefs to cookbook authors, from food magazine editors to cooking show hosts. So how does she get them to choose her client as a guest over someone else? By making sure she has a strong pitch that communicates what's unique about that chef versus all the others out there. Are his casseroles crowd-pleasers? Is she a whiz with whipped potatoes? Are they turning the farm-to-table trend on its side?

When you're trying to promote yourself, the last thing you want to do is blend into the background or be seen as nothing special. In this chapter, we'll share ideas and strategies for breaking through the clutter to make sure you get noticed.

**News Flash:
Stand out for outstanding
opportunities**

According to Karen Robinovitz of the cosmetics company Purple Lab, "It's all about presentation—remember that, when you're trying to cut through the clutter, so is everyone else. What would stand out when you present a resume, writing samples, an idea, or a presentation? How can you do something no one else will do? When I was working on my book proposal [for] a tome about fashion, I wrapped it in fishnets and sent it in Manolo Blahnik shoe boxes. It was no ordinary proposal. A book deal came three weeks later!"

The Takeaway: Tapping into your creativity can make all the difference when you're trying to stand out.

First Impressions Count

No one really knows who coined the phrase, "You never get a second chance to make a first impression," but it could easily have been a publicist. You have only about a tenth of a second to impress someone, according to research done in 2006 by Princeton psychologists Janine Willis and Alexander Todorov, and reinforced by a March 2009 study from Harvard University and New York University, which revealed that, when encountering someone for the first time, we are often quick to judge whether we like that person or not. In public relations, we try to stack the cards in our clients' favor by doing our research, helping them craft their stories, training them to project confidence, and to use the right body language.

When you meet people for the first time, how long does it take *you* to get a sense of whether you find them interesting? What strikes you about them right away?

Are they well put together or are they slovenly? Do they seem warm and approachable or standoffish? Trustworthy or phony? Are they dressed appropriately for the occasion? Does their appearance inform your opinion of them? How about the conversation? Are they instantly engaging or boring?

Most of us are able to read people quickly and determine whether we care to learn more about them. Here are some steps you can take to ensure that you will be that person whom others would like to get to know better.

 Sound Bite

"Don't pay any attention to what they write about you. Just measure it in inches."
—Andy Warhol

Stay Top-of-Mind

One of our goals as publicists is to remain top-of-mind for reporters and producers when they need to interview someone for a story. Whether we achieve that by regularly sending them press releases about our latest news, dropping them notes when we like their stories or segments, or reminding them about our clients' expertise, we do our best to stay on their radar screen so that when they have a breaking news story and need a talking head, we're first on their call list. The trick is to do this without being too aggressive and annoying. You don't want to be like those irritating salespeople who hound you by phone or e-mail, desperate to get you to buy their product (thank heaven for caller ID and junk mail folders!). This is about the "soft sell"— pitching yourself in a friendly, assertive, but not pushy way.

Some tips on how can you stay top-of-mind for potential employers, clients or even your current boss include:

- **Thinking of you.** Simply staying in contact with people can often be the thing that gets noticed. When we see a compelling article that we think a client or our boss would like to read (whether it's relevant to their industry or a more personal interest like photography or wine), we send it to them with a note saying "Thought you'd be interested..." It's an easy way to show them that you're always thinking about them, even when you're "off duty."

- **Flattery will get you everywhere.** There is a real art to complimenting others without seeming like a total brownnoser. For example, if your superior won an industry award or you read a profile of someone you'd like to work for (or with), congratulate them. No need to send flowers or spend a lot of money; a brief, well-crafted note will do. Or, if you know the person, pick up the phone and make a personal call to tell them how impressed you are— most people will appreciate the extra effort.

- **Share the good news.** This is where the classic PR skills really come in handy. It's incredibly important to make your contacts aware of *your* achievements. For example, if you're speaking on a panel, be sure to invite contacts to attend as your guests. If you just launched a new product, send a note or press release to potential buyers. If you're celebrating a milestone at your job, send your boss a note or drop it into conversation that you're excited about your fifth anniversary, biggest deal yet, etc.

Don't Be Afraid to Be Different

As Coco Chanel once said, "In order to be irreplaceable, one must always be different." And, by different, we don't mean odd (although that does work for some!). Figure out what differentiates you from the rest, and highlight it in all you do. According to HARO's Peter Shankman, one of the best pieces of career advice he ever received was "Don't be afraid to be different—you always notice the Lamborghini, not the Honda Civic." Fashion publicist Shaun Lee Lewis adds, "You know yourself better than anyone can tell you. Some things work for some people that don't work for others. Recognize, cherish, and strengthen these traits."

In PR, we work with clients to find their key differentiators or a USP (unique selling proposition); in other words, what makes them better than other brands or people in the marketplace. We develop messages around those and then incorporate those points into anything and everything we do.

Have a Signature

We talked a bit about this in Chapter 6, but having a "signature" isn't solely style-related. There are other ways to be unique and memorable. For example, Lindsey Pollak is a best-selling career advice author, Gen Y expert, and well-known cupcake enthusiast. Cupcakes, in particular, are a big part of her brand. What started as a simple dessert served at a birthday party has become a signature element on her blog, her seminars, and media interviews. And then there's *Harper's Bazaar* editor-in-chief Glenda Bailey, who always sends handwritten notes on her personal stationery to thank people for their hard work, gifts, etc. In a world of e-mail, it's refreshing and special to receive one of these cards from a busy, important woman such as Bailey.

Entrepreneur Sheryl Victor Levy takes it one step further. She suggests writing on unique stationery to make it more memorable: "When I've really wanted a job, I've sent thank-you notes on Wonder Woman cards. They're out of print now, but I always look for them on eBay and Amazon and buy them at whatever price they are. They got me my job at the interactive firm I used to work at in Boston." Another idea: Instead of sending flowers or a gift card as a thank you when someone helps you out, give them something that means a lot to you or represents your background, such as an inscribed copy of your favorite book, or some chicory coffee from New Orleans, for example, if you hail from there.

Be Creative

In our profession, you have to constantly think of creative ways to get your pitch/client/product noticed by the public and the media. From special mailings to publicity stunts, we've done it all. One Valentine's Day, Jessica—then head of PR for The Knot, an online wedding resource—sent a business re-porter a dozen mini-brownies adorned with heart-shaped stick-ers bearing the site's logo. While the journalist didn't write an immediate story about her company, he said it was the most memorable gift he'd ever received from a publicist, and they are still friendly today, a decade later.

Beauty PR pro Sheila Munguia used both creativity and a sense of humor to deal with a very important member of the media who wrote about an event she had organized. "She made a silly comment about the fish we served at lunch. Rather than get annoyed, I sent her a huge fish bowl, full of red Swedish fish candies, tied with a gorgeous, red bow with a note. She loved that I had a sense of humor, and it made us instantly connect. She supported my brand for years to come, and always gave me attention when I came to her with story ideas because she knew I was creative and 'got' her."

Years ago, public relations consultant Elizabeth Dye re-ally wanted a job at a publishing company, but the head of the department was concerned that she had jumped around too much and might not stay long, if hired. To lobby for the position, Elizabeth sent her potential boss a daily delivery of holiday candy (it was right before Christmas) with custom-ized hang-tags created by her graphic designer husband that expressed how much she wanted to work there. It was creative, memorable and—guess what?—it worked. Elizabeth was hired and stayed at the company for several years. Yes, she had the talent and experience to get the job, but it was her ingenuity, creativity, and persistence that won over her interviewer.

 News Flash: Alec Brownstein's "The Google Job Experiment"

Alec Brownstein, a copywriter at Young & Rubicam New York, was looking to land a new job. After Googling the creative directors he most wanted to work for, he realized that if someone were to put an ad targeting them above the search results for their name, they would probably notice (and, let's be honest, who doesn't Google themselves these days?). In what he calls "The Google Job Experiment," Brownstein bought ads targeting five creative directors that listed his Website's URL and read "Hey, So-and-So! Googling yourself is a lot of fun. Hiring me is fun, too." He secured interviews with four of them, received job offers from two, and now works for one of the best ad agencies in New York. Total cost of this campaign? Six dollars. Not to mention that his creative idea won him several advertising awards and international press attention everywhere from CNN to BBC.

The Takeaway: You don't have to spend a lot to get people's attention.

Another example: A young, ambitious, aspiring magazine editor named Anna Brand (great name, right?) who, in the quest to find a job as an editorial assistant in the New York magazine business, took out an ad on Facebook targeting people with a connection to magazines. She linked to her Website (*http://web.me.com/annabrand/*), which features her well-designed resume, writing samples, and contact information. Instead of just blanketing publishing companies with her resume, she spent a small amount of money ("as little as $1 a day," says Brand) to promote herself in a modern, clever way. According to Brand, "I realized that after graduating jobless, even with a magazine journalism degree, and two national editorial internships, I needed to do something more to get noticed. I started my blog, BRANDED, signed up for Twitter, became more active on LinkedIn, and once I had [more than] 30 published writing samples, began building my Website, which features all of my clips. I realized that I had to give myself the attention I deserved, rather than waiting around for someone to put the spotlight on me."

News Flash: Find a champion

Stacey Blume, designer and founder of Blume, a fun clothing company that specializes in personalization with name patches, shares how finding a champion make a difference:

"We launched Blume in December 2002. My sister knew Jennifer Lopez's stylist so she sent a pair [of our personalized underwear]. This was at the height of the 'Bennifer' phenomenon and apparently Jen went nuts for them. She ended up requesting a week's worth of 'Ben' undies. I was very fortunate that the day my Website went live was the same day that *People* magazine and the *TODAY Show* reported that celebrity Blume scoop. The hits gave my brand new company instant recognition and credibility, which had a great snowball effect. A Los Angeles radio station called to interview me and a bunch of high-end boutiques called to pick up the line."

The Takeaway: In PR, as well as in any business, one well-connected fan can make a difference. Go out of your way to identify and engage potential advocates, whether you're an entrepreneur promoting your product or an employee vying for a promotion.

"A Little Bribery Doesn't Hurt" *...and Other Ways to Attract Positive Attention*

In publicity, you often have to pull out all the stops to get noticed. Here are some of our tried and true techniques:

- **A way to anyone's heart is through his/her stomach.** We've been known to send baked goods or bottles of bubbly to reporters or producers with a pitch, and it definitely helps to get their attention. And, before every Fashion Week, Meryl's team would send bottles of vodka or rum to key editors to keep the brand top-of-mind for any after-party coverage. While it didn't always directly correlate brands to immediate coverage, it helped generate significant long-term goodwill for the brand—and the team. Jessica even once sent a reporter a package of Brick cheese, which can only be found in his home state of Wisconsin, after visiting her in-laws there. He was very appreciative!

- **Be a mentor.** We're big believers in having mentors (we both have had them throughout our careers) and, in turn, mentoring others who need advice and support. You can either do this with a younger employee at your company, through a professional organization, or even with a high school or college student looking to enter your field after graduation. Not only does being a mentor make you look good but you also never know where someone is going to end up, so taking time to help a budding superstar may come back to you in spades. Who knows? They may even hire you someday!

- **Put in the time—and watch the clock.** It's cliche to say, but face time still counts. Clients take note when you respond promptly to their messages. Bosses notice when you arrive early and/or stay late at work. All that extra time can pay off, particularly if you're able to meet deadlines; even better if you can get your projects done before they're due. Give yourself a false deadline of a day or two early—then when you get closer, you'll be further along. That way, you'll have the extra time to make sure the work is really perfect before the actual deadline arrives.

Your Personal PR Action Plan

1. Come up with three creative ways to reach out to a potential employer/client/mentor that will

break through the clutter and represent who you are. This does not have to cost a lot of money and, in fact, shouldn't.

2. **If you already have a job, challenge yourself to come in early for an entire week** and see how much more you get done, or finish at least one project before its deadline.

PROTECT

"Do not protect yourself with fences, but rather your friends."
—Liz Smith

Chapter 8
Toot Your Own Horn (but Not Too Loudly)

*"The less you speak of your greatness,
the more shall I think of it."*
—Oscar Wilde

It's our job as publicists to raise awareness and buzz for what or whom we represent, but there's a fine line between not getting enough attention and attracting too much. We all know people who constantly talk about themselves and how successful or busy they are, or how many friends they have on Facebook. But there's an art to self-promotion and part of it is building your image slowly and strategically so you don't come across as too in-your-face. Take Internet sensation Julia Allison, for example. She penned a dating column for *Time Out New York* until 2009, but really became known for exhaustively documenting her fabulous New York life on her blog (*http://juliaallison.com*) and using the Web—from Gawker to Twitter—to build her personal brand. She blogged about every party she attended, every guy she dated, posted innumerable pictures of herself posing with real celebrities, and attempted to get other sites—often successfully—to link to her revealingly personal posts. Not surprisingly, Allison's over-sharing quickly attracted the ire of critics for being shamelessly narcissistic.

Lesson: Somewhere between a hermit and Julia Allison is where you want to be. Sure, you could spend every waking moment blogging about your life or talking about yourself to anyone who would listen, but, often, showing is better than telling. If you're good at what you do, it will shine through the quality of your work. It's not that you shouldn't crow about your accomplishments, you should just make sure the **right** people know about them, subtly.

If you've ever watched morning television and have seen a guest plugging her book, magazine, TV show, or other project incessantly during the brief segment, you'll probably never see her on that program again. In our business, we advise clients to mention their brand or project no more than two or three times during an interview; otherwise they'll be viewed as too commercial or self-promoting. We once worked with a young woman who, in every staff meeting, announced all the interviews she had landed for her clients that week. After a while, her co-workers got annoyed—they knew she was a great "booker" and didn't need a play-by-play tally of her handiwork, which should have spoken for itself. Instead, she simply came across as boastful. Lesson: It's not necessary to hit people over the head.

In addition, it's important for your behavior to reflect your commitment and dedication to the job. It can be a PR nightmare when what a person does runs counter to what he or she says. For example, when New York Governor Eliot Spitzer—who during his political career prosecuted at least two prostitution rings—was revealed as Client 9, his actions spoke louder than his words, and led to his resignation. On a smaller scale, consider the example of an intern hired by Jessica's team a few years ago: She seemed qualified and buttoned-up during her interview, but shortly after she started, her behavior become strange and erratic. After helping out at an event one night, she proceeded to order a glass of wine from the bar. In general, we frown upon imbibing alcohol when working, but at only 19, this intern wasn't even of legal drinking age. Had she become drunk and hurt herself or gotten into a bad situation, Jessica's company would have been liable. While the intern's behavior was short-sighted and stupid, she was given another chance. Over the next few weeks, however, she started showing up late on multiple days without explanation, wearing jeans to work after being told that casual attire was prohibited, and brazenly interjecting her ideas to the PR team at another red-carpet event. Ultimately, she had to be let go.

Most people would be mortified if fired from an unpaid internship—let alone a paying job (or public office)—losing a valuable opportunity because of a lack of professionalism, judgment, and tact. Although this young woman was clearly surprised to lose her position, writing "I'm in shock right now" on her Twitter page, she did send a short, well-written thank you e-mail to everyone on the PR staff mentioning what she had learned during her short time working with them. She discovered an important lesson that will help her in future jobs: act like you appreciate and value the opportunity by showing up on time, and being conscientious and respectful of the company's culture and process.

 Sound Bite

"Helping others is the
best self-promotion."
—Peter Shankman, HARO

Show Your Value

In our business, we're valuable to our clients when we can devise a smart public relations strategy to raise awareness for their brand and initiatives, shield them from negative press, and bring them innovative ideas. We're valuable to the media when we give them interesting stories, land them juicy interviews, provide them with useful information, and make their jobs easier. People who demonstrate their contributions to their company or clients tend to get hired, promoted, and—particularly in a down market—survive a downsizing. Companies look for employees who offer a return on investment (or ROI), so you need to ask yourself:

- What can I offer?
- Do I—or am I willing to—go beyond what's in my job description?
- Am I worth what I'm being compensated (or am I worth more)?
- How productive and innovative am I and can I be more so?
- How do my work and ideas add to the bottom line?
- Are my contributions essential?

You know the old adage, "If a tree falls in a forest and no one is around to hear it, does it make a sound?" Well, you want to be certain that you're heard—and seen—making a difference at work. You could be really fantastic at your job, but if those around you don't know how valuable you are, you'll be at a disadvantage. So how do you show your value? Here are some suggestions:

- **Do some internal PR.** When we land press for our clients or company, we not only share the media reports with them, but also with our bosses and higher-ups at our company so they see the kinds of results we're getting. Any time you can quantify the fruits of your labors, it serves as a tangible record of your hard work. Offer to do a presentation showing your (or your group's) accomplishments for the quarter. Contact your internal communications department to see if they're interested in doing an interview or article for the company newsletter on one of your most recent successful projects. If you land a big client, make a key sale, or broker an important deal, send a note to the head of the company letting him or her know. It will be a reminder of your accomplishments and contributions.

- **Collect the evidence.** Don't wait until you have to pitch new business or request that promotion to compile the materials that illustrate the good work you've done. For hospitality clients, in particular, for whom testimonials move the needle, Meryl would typically do a quote sheet that features all of the best things that people have been said about them. Have you gotten a glowing e-mail lately from a client or colleague? It doesn't hurt to pull out the best parts or start a file with similar messages. At a minimum, it's great to boost your self confidence; at best, those accolades can help you win business, garner a promotion, or just gain respect at work.

- **Pat yourself on the back (just not too hard).** If you came up with an idea and feel that no one knows it was yours, there are subtle ways to slip it into conversation without seeming too self-congratulatory. For example, you can drop your client or boss a quick e-mail saying, "I'm so thrilled that you were receptive to my idea to _____, and I'm really excited to work with you to make it happen." If you feel someone else is taking the credit for your work, tread a bit more lightly (especially if the one passing it off as her idea is your superior). You can say, "That concept sounds really similar to one I presented. I guess great minds think alike. Maybe we can work on it together?" If you're on a job interview, mention a few key accomplishments that you've had in your professional or personal life that may not printed on your resume. Have you raised a ton of money for a charitable organization? Won new business for a past employer? Served as a mentor? Taught yourself how to speak a second language? You can broach them by saying, "I'd love to talk about a few things I'm most proud of..."

- **Pat others on the back (as hard as you'd like).** Showing value in the workplace isn't just about what you personally do. If you supervise staff or outside vendors, or work on a team, make it a point to compliment others for their contributions. Did someone in your group make you look good, come up with an idea that saved your butt, or help you meet the deadline on a project? Give credit where credit is due. Thank him or her and, even better, do it in front of an audience or to the person to whom you both report. You will be viewed as a team player, and the people you praise will be more apt to have your back in the future.

- **Bring it!** Like the cheerleading movie, you want to give it your all every day. Be active, not passive. Show positivity and enthusiasm. If it takes an extra cup of coffee in the morning to get your energy level up (as is the case with most of us!), so be it. People notice when you have fire in your belly and excitement about what you're doing. Make it your goal to bring in new business, see a big idea to fruition, manage a challenging project, update your company's Website, etc. Be a "rainmaker"—defined by Merriam-Webster as "a person whose influence can initiate progress or ensure success"—and you will undoubtedly be seen as an asset to your company.

The Art of Negotiation

One vital skill in the PR world is the ability to negotiate. When we develop good relationships with the media, and we bring them something juicy, we often try to leverage our information to secure what we want—whether it's for the news to break on a certain day, better or bigger placement of the story or broadcast interview, or accompanying artwork. Sometimes it works and sometimes it doesn't, but as Jessica's mother always advised her growing up, "The worst someone can say is no." The same goes for asking for what you want at work. Maybe you'd like more responsibility, a bigger paycheck or title, flex time, professional training, etc. Chances are, it's not just going to be handed to you, but if you consider yourself a valuable employee, attractive job candidate, or talented contractor, go after what you desire. Some of these public relations tactics can apply to anyone:

- **Make your case.** In PR, we always want to be able to back up our claims with facts. Before asking for what you want, prepare to offer reasons for why you deserve it. Research the market to find out the compensation level commensurate with your experience and field of expertise so you can negotiate a starting salary at a new job. If you're asking for a job share, offer examples of other share situations that are working at your company. Before Jessica came back from maternity leave, she asked her boss if she could work two days a week from home. She offered the following reasons for why this arrangement would work: she had a 10-year history at the company; had successfully worked from home five days a week during a five-month, doctor-prescribed period of bed rest during her pregnancy; had a remote work phone and laptop at home which enabled her to operate as if she were at the office; and was willing to be flexible about coming in on days when she was needed at work. The end result? They compromised. Jessica was permitted to telecommute one day a week—and it worked out for everyone.

- **Tit for tat.** If we offer a reporter an exclusive interview or breaking news that other outlets would want, we have the leverage to request a nice piece of real estate in their publication. They get something from us and, in return, we get something from them. If you want a raise or a promotion, be prepared to take on more responsibility, managing additional projects or people, for example. If you want your company to pay for your cell phone or Blackberry, you may have to make yourself available for work calls and e-mails during off hours. It's all about give and take.

- **Have something in your hip pocket.** If you ask for what you want and you get rejected, have a backup idea. For example, we know celebrity publicists who will pitch an up-and-coming client for the cover of a magazine only to be turned down because the person isn't big enough to sell many. So rather than strike out completely, they'll negotiate to give the magazine an A-list client if the publication agrees to run a smaller inside story or spread on one of their B-listers. It happens all the time, and both parties win. If during your performance review, you ask for a salary increase and your boss says no, have another request on deck—more vacation time, a one-time bonus, or another review in three months time—so you come out of the meeting with more than you had coming in.

 **Key Message:
Find the win-win**

According to Linda Descano of Women & Co., "Today's workforce is much more collaborative versus competitive. It's important to look for a 'win-win' versus someone winning/someone losing."

News Flash:
Proactive with passion

When Maggie Gallant, now senior vice president at Rogers & Cowan, started her own agency years ago, she went after clients she was passionate about.

"I thought about what I wanted to tell people. And I thought of Luna Bar. I was excited about [their product], so I just called and told them what I could do for them. It's that simple. You can just know that if you have the faith in yourself and can do the best job for them, tell them and back it up."

The Takeaway: If you see a good idea and/or smart people out there, don't be afraid to reach out. It can result in new business, a job, or a connection that might help down the road.

What's the Magic Word?

There's a reason saying thank you is one of the first things we learn as children—and it never gets old. Whether it's verbal, hand-written, or via e-mail, a simple thanks goes a long way. When we're happy with an article or a segment, we send a thank-you note to the reporter or producer immediately after. Helen Gurley Brown, the famous former editor-in-chief of *Cosmopolitan*, has always believed in sending personal typewritten notes and never fails to send one to thank people for even the smallest gesture. In fact, she came out with a wonderful little book in 2004 called *Dear Pussycat: Mash Notes and Missives from the Desk of Cosmopolitan's Legendary Editor*, filled with personal notes she has sent to everyone from politicians and writers to actors and socialites throughout her long career. One chapter is dedicated solely to her thank-you notes—they are not only a great read, but also a lesson in writing a memorable message! Jessica has received a couple over the years from the legendary editor, which she will cherish forever.

We believe in erring on the side of thanking people for their help, even if it didn't take much effort on their part. One of our friends asked us to meet with his boss's sister, who was in

PR but not happy at her current job. During the interview, this young woman was friendly, buttoned-up, and seemed appreciative. We even introduced her to a few colleagues who might be able to help her find a new position. However, after we'd taken time out of our busy day to meet with this woman as a favor, we never received a thank-you note—not even by e-mail—which left us with a bad impression.

People often ask us whether they should send a thank-you note via e-mail or snail mail after an interview. In this world of instant gratification, younger job-seekers often think an electronic note that arrives same-day is preferable in case an employer is making a quick decision. There's nothing wrong with that approach. However, we still see value in the handwritten note—it's a bit more formal, but also has a personal touch. Our advice: Do both. You can't go overboard being gracious.

A Little Humility Goes a Long Way

Writer Helen Nielsen once said, "Humility is like underwear, essential, but indecent if it shows." There is something to be said for having modesty. People don't want to hear you tout your accomplishments in a way that seems boastful or crass. Look at Bill Gates: he's one of the richest, smartest, most successful businessmen in the world, but unlike that other famous business mogul, Donald Trump, he doesn't go around telling people how great he is. His track record speaks for itself. That's not to say that he shuns all attention. He does the occasional interview, speaking engagement, and commercial, and gives tons of money to charity through the Bill & Melinda Gates Foundation. Of course, everyone knows who Bill Gates is and the mark he's made on the technology world, so you could say that he can afford to be humble (frankly, he can afford pretty much anything!); but you can still make an impression without yelling about yourself from every mountaintop. Do you want to be like Heidi Montag or Kate Gosselin, reality TV stars who

need their every move (and plastic surgery procedure) docu-
mented and covered by the media? Or do you want to be more
like Tom Hanks and Meryl Streep, who pick and choose their
media moments and genuinely seem like nice, unpretentious
people, even though they're world-famous actors? Here are
some tips on how to stay humble:

- **Try not to talk about yourself in the third person.** People who refer to themselves by their own
  name instead of simply using "I" can come across
  as pompous and affected. It's called *illeism* and has
  been committed by many famous people—from
  Vice President Joe Biden to former Utah Jazz player Karl Malone. It's irritating when the famous do
  it, but even worse from a regular Joe.

- **Accept the accolade.** Feel self-conscious when you
  receive a compliment or someone calls out your
  success? Having someone tout your achievements
  is truly the best kind of publicity, but how you respond can help or hinder. We probably don't need
  to tell you that saying "Yeah, that was great, wasn't
  it?" will make you sound full of yourself. More likely, the response would be something like, "Oh, it
  was nothing"—also not a good choice, as it down-
  plays the effort you exerted. Even if it doesn't come
  naturally to say it, you can strike the right balance
  with a good old "thank you."

- **Don't be afraid to ask for help.** It's okay to seek
  counsel from people who know more than you or
  have different strengths. Part of humility is admitting that you aren't good at everything, and being
  open to learning from the wisdom of others.

- **Allow yourself to make mistakes—and learn from
  them.** Everyone stumbles sometimes, and the errors we make can humble us. That's actually a good

thing because, through them, we realize we are not invincible and can draw upon our experiences to become better at what we do. We'll talk a bit more about recovering from setbacks in Chapter 11.

News Flash:
Realize you have
something to learn

Alexander Samuelson, who works in public affairs for the banking industry, learned about humility at his first job: "My first employer taught me to write a business letter, and he took the time to mentor me to do so. I didn't know how to write one, and I needed to learn it. It's a balance: You need to be aggressive, optimistic, and promotional, but you do need to be humble in that you're asking other people for things—for example, a client is paying you money, a reporter doesn't *need* to write your story."

"Being Nice Doesn't Mean Being Weak"
...and Other Ways to Get Ahead in Business

In our business, we've learned that:

- **Nice doesn't mean weak.** You don't have to be mean to get ahead; nice people can be strong, respected, and great leaders as well. In the workplace—whatever your job or interest—it's often about community, compromise, and communication. We ascribe to the "firm but friendly" approach to PR; this means that we'll do our best to resolve a situation—within reason. For example, when photographers or journalists want to cover the red carpet at a high-profile event, often we can only allow access to some of them, due to space limitations or restrictions put in place by celebrities attending the event. Frequently, those who feel that they deserve or require access will complain or threaten to not work with us again. In those instances, we'll hold our ground when necessary, and do our best to offer alternative options—but in as nice a way as possible. While you may not have occasion to deal with paparazzi (trust us, it's better that way!), responding to any annoying situation with a calm, amiable approach enables you to let people down easy.

- **Sweet = savvy.** As the old saying goes, you catch more flies with honey than you do with vinegar. For example, a customer service representative we know once told us that when disgruntled callers are rude to her, she puts them on hold and files her nails until she's ready to pick up the phone again. Instead of yelling, ask these people for their names, thank them for their help, and, in most cases, they'll be more likely to want to assist you. When reporters make a mistake, we work hard to keep our cool because we can't let anger affect our relationship. On the flip side, we've both dealt with media who have expressed disappointment that we gave a story to their competition, but if they're nice about it, we are more apt to come to them first in the future. Next time you're ready to lash out at work, remember that a kind approach will get you further than being mean.
- **Do unto others as you would have others do unto you.** There's a reason why this moral code has been around since Biblical days. If you want people to treat you with respect, treat them with respect. If you want others to help you out, lend them a hand. If you ask someone to cover your work when you're taking a mental health day, offer to reciprocate when they're feeling burned out.
- **Share the love.** If someone recommends a potential hire, a cool new restaurant, or a tip on a great sample sale, return the favor. Next time you're going out for coffee and a coworker seems snowed under, offer to grab her a grande latte on you. We've sent each other many resumes over the years when either of us was hiring, and have shared media contacts with one another that have helped us land press for our respective clients. Says marketing exec Melissa Hobley, "Go above and beyond when you are asked to help someone or do a favor. The reason it's important is that you create a reputation for yourself—not to mention karma—if you're being helpful."

Your Personal PR Action Plan

In the next week, make it a goal to toot your own horn in one or more of the following ways:

1. **Compile your own quote sheet.** Look back on e-mails to see what positive things people have said to you about your work, a project, a client, etc. Update it regularly and be sure to take a look when you're walking into an important meeting, or when you need a pick-me-up.

2. **Practice negotiating.** Whatever your goal is—whether to get a new job, move up in the one you have, or bring in new business—come up with your wish list for what you want and then rehearse what you'd say if you get a no. For example, if you get a job offer at a lower salary then you expected, walk through how you would go about negotiating for a higher figure. What if you have a client who wants to hire you, but lowballs you on a budget? How about if your boss nixes your request for a promotion?

Chapter 9
Brush Up on Your Social (Media) Studies

"If you reveal your secrets to the wind, you should not blame the wind for revealing them to the trees."
—*Kahlil Gibran*

Remember when social media was simply passing notes to your best friend in class? What about when that message accidentally fell into the wrong hands, and the word got out about a secret crush or a person you didn't like? Did you cringe as your private thoughts spread like wildfire on the playground or through the whole school, maybe even the community? Painful as that was, no doubt it's exponentially worse today; messages, images, gossip, and information can be shared with countless people in countries around the globe—within minutes—thanks to the proliferation of social media and the blurred lines between public and private.

The very best lesson we learned when *our* clandestine message was confiscated by a teacher (and all of our friends and that certain special someone subsequently found out that we thought he was "cute") was that we "shouldn't put anything down in writing that we wouldn't want published on the front page of the *New York Times*." Words of wisdom from a fourth grade teacher still ring

151

true, though it's clearly easier said than done today. It's just so simple to add those vacation photos to Facebook or whip out a quick quip about hating work (or whatever) as your Facebook status. The big difference is that, back when the news would break just on the playground—or the *Times* for that matter—people would talk and then the hubbub would die down. Now we live in a world where things spread instantaneously and can live on the Internet forever.

 Sound Bite

"Be careful of everything you write
or videotape about yourself—
your tweets, Facebook, even if
you're checking in via Four
Square or Facebook Places
in the middle of the night from a bar.
Think about yourself as a public figure.
Treat that public figure with respect because
you want to get respect back."
—Laurel Touby, mediabistro.com

Even When It's "Off the Record," It's on Your Permanent Record

In PR, we use the term "off the record" (OTR) when working with media; it's an agreement between publicists or interviewees and journalists that—though we're providing specific information—it will be used merely as background or without attribution in the article or report. Of course, today, when information can shoot from here to Timbuktu in the blink of an eye, it's harder and harder to keep those lines drawn. Take for example President Obama's off-handed criticism about Kanye West's antics at the 2009 MTV Video Music Awards, made while being miked for a TV interview. Interestingly, the time before an official interview—pre-tape chatter—has long been an unwritten OTR moment for White House reporters. In the age of Twitter, the rules are changing, and the boundaries shifting. A reporter tweeted the comment and, though it was deleted an hour later, the news had already spread.

The lesson? Just because it starts as a private conversation, photo or otherwise, doesn't mean it will end up that way. Can you say Paris Hilton (or Kim Kardashian, Pamela Anderson and Rebecca Gayheart, to name a few others)? Talk about a private—and intimate—moment caught on tape that ultimately became extremely public with millions upon millions of people watching and passing it along. But it doesn't have to be a sex tape; a cursory look at celebrity-gossip outlets such as *TMZ* and *Extra* help underscore the fact. Today, simply going to buy milk or walk a dog moves from private to public realm at lightning speed for celebs.

Private Eyes—They're Watching You

You're likely saying, "Okay, they are celebrities and *choose* to live life under the microscope for all the world to see." We would argue: Though you probably don't have paparazzi following you at every turn, by putting information out in the social media realm, you are choosing that same public life. And unfortunately, what you do can come back to haunt you. What you post on Facebook or Twitter creates your online resume. Even something as innocuous as vacation photos can have ramifications—what if you called in sick the day the image was time-stamped for and your boss happens to catch your mistake? Instead, consider each and every piece of information you put out there. Knowledge is power, and you want to be the one holding the cards.

Do you wonder how celebrities such as George Clooney or Gwyneth Paltrow typically navigate those waters better than others? Well, in most cases, celebrities like them have high-powered publicists to manage their "brand" and "likeness" closely. From a walk along the red carpet to a post-meltdown spin, these publicists are behind-the-scenes orchestrating what's disseminated with the rigor and strategy of a well-oiled military maneuver. If you want to have star power, you've got to find a way to avoid—or at least minimize—the tarnish. How do you do that? By paying attention to what you put out there and understanding that anything you share online is fair game. Before posting comments, images or video, think like a publicist would about a client. Ask yourself:

- Am I putting my best foot forward? Is what I'm doing online keeping with my personal image or brand?
- Who can see or read what I am posting/sending?
- Will people/companies want to be affiliated with this image?
- Ten or more years from now, will I still be proud of myself for that comment or my actions?

It's a known fact: HR folks are hitting Google to do a little due diligence before bringing a candidate in or making that offer. According to an August 2009 Harris Interactive/CareerBuilder survey, among the top reasons for rejecting job candidates were "provocative or inappropriate photographs or information" and "information about drinking or controlled substances" found online. That said, we know from the rising number of news stories to this effect: Candidates are also hindered by negative postings about their previous employers and other faux pas.

So how can you manage your own online reputation? In addition to being cognizant of what you and others you know are posting online about you, make sure you're checking online (via Google, Pipl, etc.) for any mention of your name, including contact information, personal and professional profiles, public records, blog posts, documents, and Web pages. Is it scary that so much information about you is easily accessible with a simple online search? Yes—but all the more reason why you should periodically do searches like this on your own name so you can see what anyone else can find out about you on the Internet. If there's something erroneous or damaging that comes up, you must be vigilant about trying to get it corrected or removed. That requires some work but, depending on how potentially damaging the incorrect information is, it could be worth the effort.

 News Flash:
Be careful about social
media overexposure

Jessica recalls a potential candidate whose online presence was his downfall: "A few years ago, a candidate came in to interview for a position with my department and on his resume he had listed the URL for his MySpace page. After the interview, we immediately went onto the MySpace page and found some very disturbing personal information (including things like 'I enjoy sexual deviance') and inappropriate, half-naked photos. Needless to say, we did not extend an offer."

The Takeaway: Be careful in general about what you put on your social media pages—which are easy enough to find with a simple Google search—but if you choose to ignore that advice, don't make it easy for your potential employer to find them by printing your URLs on your resume!

◆ ◆ ◆ ◆

"Funny pics of that orgy I went to"...and other
things not to post on your social media pages

- **NSFW photos.** Not Safe for Work or NSFW images— those that would be deemed inappropriate or racy— are the most likely to get you crossed off a short list of candidates or escorted out the door. For proof, you needn't look further than the various recently ousted beauty queens to know that images can come back to haunt you. Rule of thumb: If you wouldn't want your grandmother, father, or elementary school teacher to see them, don't post 'em.

- **Negative comments.** A recent Harris Poll found that 35 percent of HR professionals discounted candidates who were caught bad-mouthing past employers on social media sites such as Twitter and Facebook.
- **Personal information.** Though not a PR-specific rule and seemingly harmless, be wary of posting too much personal or nostalgic information about yourself online. To share your favorite movie or first pet's name could open you up to scrutiny—not to mention identity thieves—who can mine your social media profiles for information to access your various banking and credit card accounts.
- **Proprietary ideas/projects.** While the crowd-sourcing trend is alive and well, you want to be careful about putting out ideas/projects without protection. As we've discussed, ideas and information spread like wildfire and, because you can't copyright an idea, it's best to bake something a little more before putting it out to the world. Likewise for private information about your company or its clients; for most, that would be grounds for immediate termination.
- **Other people's business.** Just as you're looking to manage your image and information online, understand that your friends, family, and coworkers must do the same. Be sensitive and respectful; don't just post photos or information about them without giving them fair warning, or you could inadvertently or innocently do damage. Someone posted a photo of our friend standing next to a guy smoking pot from years ago.

While our pal wasn't actually toking up, he was none too thrilled that the image was there for all 800 of his "friends" to see and immediately asked the person to remove it.

If You Don't Have Anything Nice to Say...

In the movie *Steel Magnolias*, a great examination of inter-personal relationships and the cycles of life among a group of Southern women, one of the characters, Claree, elicits guffaws with the line, "If you don't have anything nice to say, come sit next to me." We laugh, because it is easy—even fun some-times—to complain about people or things. All you have to do is look at the TV lineup to find shows like *Gossip Girl* or peruse magazines such as *Us Weekly* and blogs like *PerezHilton* to get a clear understanding that gossip continues to hold a significant place in our lives. Just know that, even if said in jest, nega-tive comments have a habit of coming back to bite you in the butt—be it online or in real life. Consider the California Pizza Kitchen employee who tweeted about the "lame" change in uniforms, only to find himself out of the kitchen for good.

**News Flash:
Customer satisfaction
is just a click away**

According to celebrity blogger Micah Jesse Koffler founder of Micahjesse.com, you can use social media to promote brands that you use, love, and want to connect with.

"I once tweeted I was going to McDonald's to pick up one of their delicious McCafé beverages and, just a few hours later, I received an e-mail from the marketing manager for McDonald's introducing herself and thanking me for being a fan, and then sent me a pack-age a few weeks later with gift cards for free McCafé beverages."

Social media guru Peter Shankman shared a similar story. "I'm a huge frequent flier on Continental. I never check bags when I travel but, about a few months ago, I did. Of course, they lost it. I tweeted about it; the baggage was found and on its way back to me within a half hour. They were listening and that's what is key now to good customer service."

The Takeaway: It's easier than ever to connect with consumers; just be sure to listen and respond quickly.

Positive Reinforcement

All these warnings don't mean that we want you to shut down your social media efforts and disconnect your WiFi. To be relevant in today's marketplace (and even in the dating scene, mind you), an online presence is non-negotiable. According to a poll by social media site Mashable.com, over 45 percent of employers now proactively screen social media profiles. As mentioned, when evaluating job candidates, the first bit of vetting happens online via Google and other search engines. How to you make sure that the "cream" of your information rises to the top? Put your positive information out there on a regular basis. Do you have a Website or blog? Are you active on social media (and not only when you need a job)? How do you sell yourself when you're not there in person to do so? And how do you manage your online reputation?

For those looking for a consulting job or project, your gig could come from anywhere. Be sure that your key messages are clearly communicated via a variety of outlets. Starting your own Website or blog is a low-cost and easy way to position yourself and forge the best communication with your audience. Joining online communities that will allow you to network and get your name out is also important. On your favorites sites or blogs, be a frequent commenter on stories you like or disagree with and offer to write a guest post. Popular sites like the *Huffington Post* are open to taking blog entries from various personalities on all sorts of topics. We've had our clients post their takes on a particular subject on HuffPo, and they always yield a ton of response. Seed your ideas and images via your LinkedIn profile, include your elevator pitch and contribute to industry applicable discussions to reinforce your relevance and expertise.

If you're seeking a new job, you must be social media savvy—have a Facebook and Twitter presence, use LinkedIn to network and, where applicable, have your own blog. Even a Tumblr or Flickr account, which are very easy to set up, can help underscore your understanding of the digital media realm. List yourself on Twitter directories such as Twellow and We Follow, where you can also search for people to follow in categories of interest that may help you with your job search or make connections. Keep in mind that social media is a two-way conversation. If you communicate with others in your network versus merely sitting back and observing other people's conversations, it will benefit you more.

Integrate Social Media Into Your Life

According to Michael Lazerow, CEO of social networking company Buddy Media, "The best way to use social media is to commit to it and be social from the beginning. Look at social media as something that's just a part of your life. You put yourself out there in a very real way. You share information, you share advice, you comment and engage like a real person, and by the time you go to change jobs or find a job, you have a footprint or social identity. The worst thing you can do is decide once you need a job, you sign up for LinkedIn and Facebook then and potential employers go to look for you online and you have three friends on Facebook, a couple on LinkedIn and no one follows you on Twitter."

Says Steve Farnsworth, chief digital strategist for Jolt Social Media, "For the most part, social media only has anecdotal accounts of helping people find a job, but that's okay because social media's real power lays elsewhere. More often than not, winning job leads are still found through personal relationships. Social media is great for meeting new people and building and nurturing relationships more deeply than ever before. Also, job offers are made after a candidate has shown the prospective employer his/her ability to get the job done. That is where social media really shines. This is your chance to have a body of work that demonstrates both thought leadership and domain expertise...an opportunity that you rarely get during a job interview."

☑ Fact Check

In a recent study, Nielsen found that, on average, about 23 percent of our online time is spent on social networking sites, versus 8.3 percent on e-mail. Facebook is dominating this space, with an 85 percent share of social networking use. (*PCWorld*, "Social Media Changes Old Web Habits" by Brennon Slattery, August 2, 2010)

According to Laurel Touby of mediabistro.com, if you can take your expertise to the Web either in the form of a blog or a Twitter account, you should create a conversation, even if it's just with yourself at the beginning. She recommends blogging or Tweeting about the people with whom you're meeting. One trick: Make it a point to ask the same question to everyone you meet with and report back. The more value you add to your Twitter account, blog, etc., the more interesting it is for others to read. And, she adds, "When the employer looks you up, they'll see the relevant information. They'll think you're smart and have contacts."

News Flash: Not all social media is created alike

Buddy Media's Michael Lazerow explains the difference among popular social media sites and how they should be used:

"You have to be cognizant of the different sites. On Facebook, you are who you are; Twitter is an information network of sharing content; LinkedIn is more for professional purposes, online resume; Pandora is for music. You have to kind of realize the same social skills that you use in real life change. If you go to a concert, you're clapping and dancing. If you go to a comedy club, you're laughing. If you use those same social skills at a funeral, you're screwed. It's the same thing [with social media]—don't show up at LinkedIn and hammer a potential business associate with 'Hey, let's get drinks.'"

Adds Jolt Social Media's Steve Farnsworth, "Look at each platform with an eye to what kind of people, and in what tone, you want to connect. I use the 'Would I have a beer with them?' grader. For me, Twitter is a cocktail party. I'll chat and connect with people who seem interesting, but I probably don't know. LinkedIn is professional. I'll connect with people I know, though it may be only superficially; basically, people I would have a cup of coffee with if they wanted advice, or we have a mutual acquaintance. For me, Facebook is for building friendships and staying connected. While they might be people I know professionally, I only connect with people I would gladly have a beer with or invite to a party. However, the best part about social media is you can make your own definition, but it is important that you have a clear strategy on how you are going to present yourself on a given platform. Sharing the wrong thing with the wrong group can cost you a job offer."

The Takeaway: Be aware of social media etiquette, know your audience and how, where, and in what way they like to receive information.

Key Messages:
Tricks of the trade from
social media pundits

- **Be authentic.** The digital generation is all about authenticity. Just look at user-generated content: it's all about being honest, open, and putting yourself out there for the virtual world to see. According to Michael Lazerow, "the best way to use social media is to—on a day-in, day-out basis—be real, be yourself, and show up with something to offer. Don't just say you're at lunch on Twitter—have some information to share. On LinkedIn, be connected to people you respect. Your network will speak for itself. The fact that you have shared friends with people on Facebook, are connected with people in your industry defines you and is an asset you bring to the business. On Facebook, your friends are real friends, not random folks. On LinkedIn, maybe people have reviewed you. All this stuff makes you real and, in my mind, social media is a stripping back of everything that's not authentic about brands and people. "

- **Use your status wisely.** No one needs to know that you just ate a marshmallow, and they certainly don't need to hear you air dirty laundry about friends or work. Instead, treat it as valuable real estate—like a billboard in Times Square for which you are paying big money—and it just might payoff big time. It did for author and career trend expert Lindsey Pollak; she was headed to Los Angeles on a personal trip and posted a note to that effect as part of her LinkedIn status. By the time her flight landed at LAX, she had a message from an *NBC Nightly News* producer who had been looking on the site for a Gen Y expert to book for the West Coast-based show. Another great example: Entrepreneur Stacey Blume used her Facebook status to share that Saks Fifth Avenue had highlighted her line. A producer at *The Rachael Ray Show* saw it and called her to provide product as a gift to actress Julianna Margulies who was going to be on the show the next day—all from a simple status update.

- **You don't need be everywhere.** Pollak encourages, "Take a look at people you admire in your space. For example, TV writers are on Facebook but don't do LinkedIn. The opposite goes for sales; if you're not on LinkedIn as much, you don't exist. Figure out what works for the industry you want and make sure your profiles reflect your goals."

- **Know your target and communicate accordingly.** There's no one best way to get noticed online because every communication can and should be tailored to each person who will see it. HARO's Peter Shankman recommends first finding out where and how your audience likes to receive information. Subscribe to RSS feeds and Websites that focus on the industry or topic to get the lay of land and understand how they communicate.

- **Protect your good name.** In PR, we set up tons of Google alerts for our clients, but Parsons' professor Tom Handley strongly recommends setting up an alert for *yourself.* "It's important to know what's being said about you in a timely manner." In fact, we recommend taking that one step further: set up a social media listening post. Do an initial search on Twitter and Google Blogs, then establish a feed to send information to a reader (Google Reader) or aggregator (TweetDeck). This saves you the time of having to go out and visit several different sites and resources because it literally pulls together the information in a single place, creating in essence a "personal newspaper." Some of them require a simple download of software, some are web-accessible; in addition, they offer different features, such as the ability to filter by category, search channel, or labels.

- **Size up your competition.** According to Pollak, now more than ever, there's a ridiculous opportunity to eavesdrop on whatever anyone else is doing; you can glean tips on what other experts in the field are doing and get to know the space. Not sure what to put on your resume? Check out the 75 million examples on LinkedIn. See what your competitors are saying about themselves, and figure out what makes you unique.

- **Pass it on.** According to Micah Jesse Koffler, an important way to build your network and get noticed online is to comment or re-Tweet VIPs' Tweets. "Starting a dialogue is a great way to get people wondering 'Who is this girl/guy and how does he/she know that person?'"

- **People who need Pipl.** If you want to find info on a specific person, such as an executive at the company where you're interviewing or a potential client, there's a site called Pipl (*www.pipl.com*) where you can type in a name and get results that include contact information, personal profiles, business and professional bios, Webpages, videos, and blog posts.

If you're able to demonstrate thought leadership in your area of expertise, it may help you get one step closer to your ultimate job. For example, Meryl's blog *Searching for Jake Ryan* (*www.searchingforjakeryan.com/blog*) highlights the best in culinary, travel, and other experiences around the world, dovetailing with her focus on lifestyle PR such as restaurants, spirits, and travel destinations. Jessica's blog—*Funny Word of the Day* (*www.funnywordoftheday.com*)—helps position her as a resource and keeps her connected to her friends in the media in a way that doesn't ask anything from them (except for, on occasion, suggestions for funny words). Our blogs let us have a dialogue with key tastemakers in a light-hearted, friendly, and non-threatening manner. That way, we're able to gain access more easily when we might need to engage them for professional reasons.

One caveat: If you already have a personal blog or are thinking about starting one, be sure to check your company's policies in place about what employees can or can't discuss. We know of cases where an employee was fired for having a personal blog that was considered a conflict of interest. Do your homework—in this market, your use of social media is not worth losing a job over.

But having a blog can also be used as a tool to get noticed—in a good way. In 2009, Amanda Casgar was eager to interview for a position as a lifestyle correspondent for a winery called Murphy-Goode in Sonoma, California. In an effort to get their attention, she started a blog called Goode Times with Amanda Casgar   (*http://goodetimeswithamandacasgar.blogspot.com/*)   to lobby for the job and expound on her personal love of wine. Her blog intro reads: "I'm a marketing geek with a love for wine. Join me as I chronicle my aggressive campaign to become the new Murphy-Goode Wine Country Lifestyle Correspondent. Nothing but Goode Times." She stated her mission and key messages right up front and her blog, Facebook group, and Twitter feed got her a lot of attention, even a front page story in the Styles section of *The New York Times*. Although she didn't ultimately land the position, she did get other opportunities as a result.

One-on-One Interview: Amanda Casgar

Q: How did you hear about the job at Murphy-Goode?

A: A friend of mine in the wine industry heard about the job from a recruiter and immediately forwarded it to me, as she knew how well suited I was to the position.

Q: How did you come up with the idea to start a blog to lobby for the position?

A: I figured I need to go full-tilt to get the attention of the company and also consumers. They conducted the job search like *American Idol* so I needed to ask America to vote in as many creative ways as possible.

Q: What did you do to get the word out?

A: I posted links on my Facebook page, I created a Facebook group, and asked all of my friends to join, I purchased an ad campaign on Facebook advertising my Goode Times with Amanda Casgar group and blog, and I started Tweeting.

Q: How did you get people to vote for you?

A: By pasting a link on my Facebook status update and sending an e-mail to my friends with instructions to forward it on to as many people as possible.

Q: Did your blog and social media campaign help land you an interview with the winery?

A: I certainly think it helped. My video was also a bit different than the competition, as I got permission from a friend who is a musician to use one of his hits as background music in the clip.

Q: How did the *New York Times* piece come about?

A: A friend writes for them, and at dinner one night, I was telling him about my campaign. He was actually inspired by me to start Tweeting as well. When he heard that a colleague was doing a piece about Tweeting for a job, he gave her my contact info. The rest just happened organically.

Q: What other opportunities has this led to?

A I've been contacted about a couple of jobs as a result of people seeing the *New York Times* piece.

Q: What did you learn from the experience?

A: Opportunities come when you put yourself out there and maximize your network. You never know who or what will lead to a break.

Q: What advice do you have for others on how to use social media to get noticed by a potential employer?

A: In this day and age, everyone can develop themselves into a brand utilizing strategic social media tools. The more creative and smart you are in developing that brand shows a potential employer that you will be equally inventive on their behalf.

Take a cue from Amanda and consider the following:

- Are there creative ways in which you can use social media to help you get your name out?
- Who is in your network and how are you communicating with them on a regular basis?
- What are your extra-curricular interests and how can you leverage them in a digital way to help you land your dream job?

If you have a job, but are looking to stand out and be recognized for your contributions and resourcefulness, keeping up with the latest technology and looking for ways to help your employer navigate the digital waters is a great way to get noticed. We've both been active in spreading the social media gospel at our respective companies. At Hearst, Jessica has held social media training sessions for various groups at the company. Meryl helped set up her former agency's Twitter and Facebook pages, and worked with the team to redesign the company's Website to optimize its searchability as a way to ensure that the company remained relevant, and continued to attract new clients and employees.

How does your company handle social media? Compare those efforts to the competition. Even better, follow the competition on social media to see firsthand how they're using it. Is there anything they're doing better? Does your own company fall short? If so, what can you offer to help close the gap? In a poll by the Council of Public Relations, more than 59 percent of respondents feel technology is under-used in public relations campaigns. An *Investment News* poll showed that a mere 14.9 percent of financial advisors say they communicate with clients or colleagues through Twitter, and only 44.9 percent and 43.8 percent of advisers say they use LinkedIn and Facebook, respectively. No doubt, those numbers are consistent with findings in other industries, including yours.

Who knows whether Twitter or Facebook will still be popular—or even obsolete—in a year, replaced by the next hot social media site or trend, but one thing is clear: social media is here to stay and, in order to be part of the conversation, you need to be up on how best to use it to your advantage.

Your Personal PR Action Plan

1. **Get your social media house in order.** What comes up in the searches on you? To push the less professional stuff to the background, beef up your newer entries with information/images you'd want a prospective client or employer to see.
2. **Photo finish.** Check out your various images on Facebook, MySpace, Flickr, etc. Is there a frat party

photo on there that you've forgotten about? Remove photos that could send the wrong message; untag those that don't live on your profile. Add newer ones and tag them so that they come up easily when Googling.

3. **Update your LinkedIn profile.** Lindsey Pollak recommends spending as much time on your LinkedIn profile as you would on your resume. Is your experience updated? What about your most recent projects? Have you updated your connections lately? Consider a few ideas for your status that might generate more attention from those searching about your industry.

4. **Tap Twitter.** If you're not on, join. Make sure you have a nice picture and easy to remember name. Use search.twitter.com to find and follow people talking about your industry. What are some tweets you can post each day to help you land that new position or client, or get noticed?

5. **Your Blog/Your Brand.** Do you have a blog? Whether personal or professional, what does it do to advance your image? Does it demonstrate core professional skills (writing, thought-leadership) or your personality in a compelling way? If you don't have one, think about starting one. Research other blogs in your industry and determine whether you can bring something new or different to the landscape.

Chapter 10

Gratification Doesn't Have to Be Instant

"The gratification comes in the doing, not in the results."
—James Dean

Do you find yourself getting annoyed by a slow-moving cashier, or irritated by the fact that you might have to wait a week for that iPad, or that you haven't received an e-mail response from a friend? We're all accustomed to the at-your-fingertips mentality that comes from a world where there's an app for almost anything and an unmatched immediacy, so it's no wonder instant gratification has become the standard rather than the exception.

We certainly appreciate the convenience that comes with a world where we no longer have to fax releases to news desks and we can manage communication from a beach on the other side of the world as easily as if we were sitting in our offices. That said, the ease of technology has also brought rise to pervasive mistakes, missteps, and general misgivings.

Even in our fast-paced work environment, we've realized that in order to get things done *correctly*, we must take the time to slow down, pay attention to the details, and have the patience to wait for the results we want.

Consider the Consequences

Before you jump into anything, consider the consequences. Think about the celebrities (Lindsay Lohan springs to mind) that seem to run off willy-nilly, only to find their mug shots splayed across the Internet and entertainment magazines for all the world to see—it's the ultimate cautionary tale. With Flip video and camera phones so widespread, there is literally nowhere for those behaving badly to hide:

- Run a red light? There's a camera to capture it.
- Send an angry e-mail? The recipient could easily circulate it far and wide in a matter of minutes.
- Even a seemingly simple stumble gets posted on YouTube at lightning speed.

We're not trying to make you paranoid (well, maybe just a little). Just know that anything you say (or do or drink) can and may be held against you in the court of public opinion. A little forward thinking will save you a lot of heartache down the road.

Particularly in an immediacy-driven environment, minor mistakes can have a major impact. Take the stock-market freefall that happened in May 2010. According to reports, the nosedive was due to a simple clerical error. What did it? The trader mistakenly typed in "b" for billion instead of inputting "m" for million. Scary when you think of the panic that set in around the world.

In clothing design and carpentry, the adage "Measure twice, cut once" is a golden rule. In PR, we simply encourage a pause before printing (or pushing the send button) as a way to limit mistakes or misunderstandings.

We both employ the "second set of eyes" rule when dealing with any communication—e-mail, press release, pitch letter, or proposal—that is sent from our offices. This means, for the important e-mails or documents, the person who wrote it engages a colleague to give it a once over before it is sent or presented. This helps eliminate careless errors and hone the language to present a more polished message. If you work solo or don't feel comfortable asking a coworker or friend to review, be your own editor by taking a break before the second look. Draft the document, print it out, and put it aside for a half hour or so. Come back and begin reviewing through from the last word/page to the first, then read it out loud from the beginning. If you stumble or it sounds awkward, it likely is. Edit and review again before sending. Although it seems tedious, that fresh set of eyes could make a big difference. Anything from your finances to your job security could depend on it.

Hit the Pause Button

Lisa Sharkey, a senior vice president at HarperCollins who frequently communicates with her authors electronically, advises: "Send every e-mail you write to both yourself and one other person you trust first to see how it feels to receive it. What's the tone? How does it come across? Also, set spell-check on your Blackberry, as well as your computer. It's easy to do and it will serve as a trick to slow you down."

Speaking of slowing down, remember when you used to count to 10 when facing an argument? How about when people draft handwritten letters and then set them aside briefly before sending—or after re-reading, decide to rip them up instead? Today, in our get-it-done-now society, it's more common to fire off a missive on a whim, which we know can prove detrimental to one's success and career trajectory.

Instead, we recommend that you hit the "pause" button before sending. Who hasn't accidentally responded to all or plugged the wrong name into the address line of an e-mail, or jotted off an e-mail that, after reading it, came across as terse or set the wrong tone?

Jessica once made the mistake of shooting off a note about an editor being a jerk, thinking she was sending it to a co-worker. About a second after hitting "send" she realized that she had e-mailed the editor instead! After attempting to recall the message (which, by the way, never really works), she immediately picked up the phone and called the guy to explain and apologize for her stupidity and unprofessional behavior. While they ended up having a frank and important conversation that cleared the air of some issues, and helped strengthen their working relationship, the way they got there was certainly not ideal.

Sound Bite

"If we are facing in the right
direction, all we have to
do is keep on walking."
—Buddhist proverb

**News Flash:
Sometimes the answer's
been there all along**

Career coach Maggie Mistal shared her own personal story of discovery and realization: "I started out by getting my accounting degree—I was solely focused on wanting to be financially independent. I knew pretty early on that it wasn't right for me: first, I like people more than numbers. Second, I'm not a detail-oriented person (two things that accountants probably shouldn't say). So, I switched to consulting at Arthur Andersen (AA), into a division called Change Enablement. I was getting warmer. While I was there, I often found myself working with colleagues to prepare for their annual reviews, helping them highlight their strengths and set goals. When AA went under, it was the biggest blessing in disguise. I had been there seven years and probably would still be there if the firm hadn't gone away. As part of the package, I was paid for about four months and decided to use that time to coach at the Life Purpose Institute. When I uncovered my own strengths/passions/interests/motivation, it pointed back to career coaching. I [then] took a job at Martha Stewart to pay bills while I developed my coaching skills. I've been the career coach for Martha and today I have my own radio show on Sirius as well as write for *Whole Living*. Once I examined it, I had been having career conversations every day for my entire professional life. I just didn't know right away how to package and leverage it."

It's a Process

As we all know, you can't just rush up Mount Everest. Even a less taxing hike needs training and preparation. You have to get acclimated at each level.

Altitude training is when endurance athletes train for several weeks at high altitude as a way to help the body adapt to the relative lack of oxygen found at that level. The body dictates the process—you have to work towards it, build up to it. It requires training, patience, time, and commitment.

At times, the PR process can be like preparing to scale Mount Everest—intense, frustrating, but, when you hit that peak—wholly gratifying. Mediabistro founder Laurel Touby agrees: "One of the things I was taught early on was that you have to treat your career very professionally—-like a salesperson. Salespeople know about rejection. You're going to make 100 calls and you might get two yeses and a couple maybes. You have to keep trying. Don't take it personally or look at it as though you're not a good person." When looking for a job or trying to find the ultimate consulting gig, she suggests filling an Excel file with 100 companies or positions that you want. "Then go one by one and realize that every single one is a possibility. You can't feel depressed if you still have 70 to go. Think, 'I can win this game. It's just a numbers game.'"

Sound Bite

"Opportunity is missed by most
people because it is dressed
in overalls and looks like work."
—Thomas Edison

Follow-up, Follow-up, Follow-up

Follow-up is like the Hallmark card of any interaction, business, or person. Doing it demonstrates that you care enough to send your very best. Stylist Sarah Shirley says that follow-up is essential in her world. She likens it to watering a plant—daily caretaking of the relationships with clients and media with whom she works.

In PR, it's imperative to follow up *and* follow through. Media people are inundated with information. We can attest to the fact that sending a press release or pitch is just the beginning. Success comes from regular, strategic, and committed check-ins. In fact, any publicist worth his or her salt has a story about the "big fish" he or she reeled in after months—even years—of pursuit. A young woman Meryl worked with had easily logged a minimum of 365 days of follow-up before landing a segment for a spirit brand's mixologist on a popular late night show. When the call came, and the show aired, it was a huge feather in her cap. Another great example: PR bigwig Heidi Krupp pitched a client to *The Oprah Winfrey Show* for two full years before she finally landed the booking—and it was for a highly coveted week-long series. Clearly, the hours of persistence paid off in those situations, but the importance of follow-up extends well beyond the world of PR. For example:

- **TV producers and journalists chase down stories with a commitment and unmatched doggedness.** They know that the story isn't going to come to them. In order to get their scoops and land great stories, they must do their research and call multiple contacts to glean the information and interviews they need.
- **Salespeople would agree that follow up is key.** If you are lucky enough to have a lead—someone who is interested in buying whatever widget or service

you're hawking—you often have to reach out to potential clients or customers several times before closing the deal.

- **Attorneys know that connecting with the client, reaching out to opposing counsel, doing endless research, and persistent follow-up is required for success in the courtroom and at your firm.** Case closed.

- **Gallery owners know that the funds are in the follow-up.** Any person who walks through the doors will often be asked for their e-mails or mailing addresses. Monthly outreach is typically done to announce an upcoming show or the appearance of a new piece by a favorite artist. That truly is the art of the deal.

Alex Samuelson, director of public affairs at a global bank, likens proactive pitching and follow-up to baseball, because you fail more often than you succeed. He says, "Baseball Hall of Famers fail seven out of 10 times. You can't get demoralized. You have to be like an actor or athlete and press on."

In fact, the late beauty industry icon Estée Lauder once said, "If you have a goal, if you want to be successful, if you really want to do it…you've got to work hard, you've got to stick to it and you've got to believe in what you're doing." Through her persistence and charm, Lauder managed to convince department stores all over the world to carry her products, even after being turned down countless times.

 Sound Bite

"Luck is not chance, it's toil;
fortune's expensive smile is earned."
—Emily Dickinson

Be Persistent Without Being a Pest

In our field, we have to strike a delicate balance between diligently following up with media and being cognizant of not annoying the heck out of them. When we pitch a reporter or producer, we try to give them a reasonable amount of time in which to respond to our idea instead of e-mailing them and then calling an hour later to see if they're interested. Persistence is important for sure, but you have to use your judgment in terms of how much follow-up is too much. For example, if we don't hear back after e-mailing or calling a member of the media three times, our idea probably didn't excite the person, and we move on.

You also don't have to use every communiqué as a selling opportunity. Sometimes just keeping in touch when you don't need something can help you when you do. In 2009, Peter Shankman did close to $200,000 in business, simply because of staying connected via Facebook. He stayed in contact by wishing others a happy birthday, acknowledging posts, or offering them assistance. "Do great things for others and *they* will become your own best publicists," he says.

Of course, there is a time when the scales are tipped and your follow-up ends up being something that other people dread. According to Kristen Angus, international communications specialist for Tourism New South Wales in Australia, "It's a fine line to walk...It's important to understand [your audience] to identify the appropriate follow-up timeframe. Don't harass the journo or they won't answer/return your call again, and are likely to file your next release in the bin!" So, you might be wondering how many calls you can make to those reporters/sales leads/recruiters before it starts to irk them. It's not necessarily the number of calls, but the content that could make the biggest impact.

For example, Meryl remembers a vendor for a media monitoring service who, no exaggeration, stalked her for more than two years. The vendor refused to hear the feedback about why her company's services were not right at the time (they really didn't have the ability to monitor media outlets unless they were online), and continued to harass Meryl and her team on a weekly basis. After getting a team member on the phone, this saleswoman launched into a 20-minute monologue about why she thought that the agency should use her services without addressing the concerns that had been expressed. Ultimately, she had to be told in no uncertain terms that the agency would not be doing business with her—ever. Had she absorbed the constructive criticism and adapted her pitch to address the firm's questions to bring additional value to the conversation, perhaps the outcome would have been different.

Scott Cooke of GCK Partners points to an ongoing relationship with a reporter from the *New York Times* as a prime example that there's a way to be persistent without being a pest. "I had been pitching a very senior editor there for months. He passed on one idea. He took a meeting with my client on another pitch (reluctantly, I suspect). On subsequent occasion, he either wasn't interested, or replied with the classic 'Thanks, I will keep in mind.' I kept up to speed on his work, knew what to pitch and how to address him and finally he responded, 'Scott, if there were an award for persistence in PR, you should win it. I'd be happy to give the speech and hand you the trophy!' He added, 'I am glad that you kept in touch, and I'm happy to take a look and learn more about your client.' He now e-mails me for advice on resources and for quotes."

The lesson: Gratification comes in many forms. It's all about listening to the other person and finding a way to address concerns or add value every time you follow up.

Key Message:
Talk it up

Stylist Erin Busbee believes that the more you share, the better your business: "I tell everyone I can about my business. Even people I barely know. I've figured out ways to work it into conversation in a short amount of time so it seems natural, not gratuitous and annoying."

Key Message:
Be passionate and patient

Producer turned publishing exec Lisa Sharkey tells us how having the patience to build a relationship over time can be worth the wait: "I realized about 20 years into my television career that I didn't want to work in TV anymore. So I followed my heart. I had always been really interested in books and had become close with so many authors through my work as a producer. I knew I had a skill that was transferable to the publishing world. One of the authors I worked with often, Jorge Cruise, introduced me to Jane Friedman, who was then CEO of HarperCollins. She wanted to know who the 'secret weapon' behind the success of his books was. I met with her and told her that I could bring an electricity from another universe [TV] into her industry. I had a great meeting with her, and she introduced me to others at the company. They said, 'You're great but we're not ready for you yet.'

I then left *Good Morning America*, where I had been a producer for five years, and went to head up Al Roker Productions. While there, I worked with Caroline Kennedy on a 50th Anniversary Special on John F. Kennedy's book, *Profiles of Courage.* That book happened to have been published by HarperCollins, so I reconnected with Jane. Then I read about HarperCollins' high-profile [departure] of Judith Regan. [I] knew that I had similar skills to her and could fill the function she had served for them. I e-mailed Jane and we went for a drink. I had just been offered the number-two job at *Inside Edition* and had verbally accepted. The first thing Jane said to me (after I spilled my glass of red wine on her!) was 'Now we're ready for you.'

After three years, the timing was finally right. So I explained the situation to *Inside Edition's* executive producer and he said,

'I don't blame you. It's a great opportunity.' I went on to help him get two book deals!"

 Sound Bite

> "One's best success comes after their greatest disappointments."
> —Henry Ward Beecher

Dealing With Disappointment

Sometimes, though, just because you put in the time, doesn't mean you're at the finish line. There are instances when disappointment comes into play, and it may be difficult for some to understand why things didn't go as you'd hoped:

- The job goes to someone else.
- You are passed over for a promotion or plum assignment.
- The account that you've been killing yourself to land goes to someone else.
- A meeting you had planned for doesn't go well.

On many occasions, we've worked with a reporter on a story, given them tons of information or access, clearly communicated our key messages, and bent over backward. Then, the piece runs or the segment airs, and the information included is wrong, the tenor of the piece is less than complimentary, or our client is marginalized or cut out of the piece altogether. Perhaps even worse: After all our blood, sweat, and tears, the piece ends up not running at all! Disappointing? No doubt. But, what top PR people do in that scenario is assess the situation and try to find a way to bounce back. They also know that, often, the best opportunities follow the greatest disappointments.

Years ago, Jessica ran PR for The Knot, and *The Oprah Winfrey Show* called her to book her editor-in-chief, and help them put together a wedding-themed show. Thrilled at the enormous opportunity, she scrambled to call in 40 wedding dresses from various designers for an engaged celebrity scheduled to appear on that episode to choose from (and arranged to have the manufacturers offer it to her for free), found women willing to share their personal wedding disaster stories, and put together wedding-planning tips for her boss to share on the program. A couple days before her company's spokesperson was set to go to Chicago, Jessica still hadn't heard from the producer about travel arrangements or last-minute details. When she called to check in, the producer informed her that Ms. Winfrey had decided to do the show without a wedding expert so they wouldn't be needing her after all. Of course, Jessica was upset—she had helped produce their entire show and was now being cut out of it. Not letting her disappointment consume her, she called the producer and insisted that, after all the work they put in, their brand be incorporated into the show in some way. Sure enough, the day the show aired, Oprah gave an on-air shout-out to Jessica's company, and the PR generated from just a mention crashed their server! Rather than wallow in her own sorrow, Jessica had been able to take a breath and ask for what she wanted. It may not have been the original plan, but it still worked.

Key Message: Push through with passion

Entrepreneur Stacey Blume believes that passion is key to make it through the challenging times. "It is easy to be excited when things are going well, so the challenge is to stay passionate during the hard times. It is important to remember that initial spark of inspiration and to try to reignite it whenever obstacles occur, because the journey of any successful venture will most likely be filled with plenty of obstacles. My advice is to just continue to believe in yourself and keep knocking (on doors)!"

◆ ◆ ◆ ◆

"I'm interested in a job in pubic relations"...
and other simple mistakes you can easily avoid

Mistakes are easy to make if you're hitting send too quickly. Here are some simple ways to sidestep an embarrassing e-mail moment:

- **Avoid grammar gaffes.** Jessica once received a cover letter from a potential job candidate that started, "I'm interested in a job in pubic relations..." Although she had obviously meant to write "public relations," her careless error made it sound as if she really wanted a job in the porn industry. Needless to say, she was not called in for an interview!

  Ever wonder why there are so many books to point out the typical grammatical errors, such as The Grouchy Grammarian, Eats Shoots and Leaves, Woe Is I: A Grammarphobe's Guide to Better English in Plain English...? Because they are, well, typical. English is a complicated language, and pop culture does its part to make correct usage sound wrong. Think about the use of "him" versus "he," or "me" versus "I," and you get the picture. We strongly recommend brushing up on your skills—get one of the books and review the basics. To get noticed or get ahead, it's essential to communicate well and knowing when to use "their" versus "they're," or "peek" versus "peak," for example, could make the difference. You're the communicator of the message—if the message is incorrect, that means you are not being effective.

- **Don't use your PDA as an excuse for poor spelling.** Make sure that you have set your Blackberry/iPhone/what-have-you to "spell." We just can't abide by the caveat seen on so many PDA message signatures, blaming the device for simple errors. While those taglines are cute (one of our favorites is "Grammatical and spelling errors brought to you by the letter 'B' for Blackberry"), it simply takes one extra moment to spell check and proofread before hitting send.

- **Make a fresh start. When it comes to crafting e-mails, we recommend starting a new message versus forwarding one to another person.** It's just too easy to inadvertently forward a message not meant for someone else's eyes. Furthermore, in starting fresh, always wait to plug in the person's e-mail address until after the message has been written and triple checked. That's the best way to avoid sending an incomplete or incorrect e-mail.

Your Personal PR Action Plan

1. **Create a "cautionary tale" file.** Fill it with examples of gaffes or missteps that you've witnessed or read about, and review it once every few weeks as a reminder to pause before hitting send.

2. **Practice your follow-up.** Don't take a lack of response as a final answer when you're reaching out to a potential employer, client, or business associate. Contact them at least twice by e-mail. If you don't hear back, pick up the phone. Sometimes it's easier to get in touch with someone that way. Most people get tons of e-mails every day, and if they don't recognize a name, they might not open it, or it may go into their junk mail folder.

3. **Invest in a grammar guide and/or a style guide.**
   Books such as *Associated Press Stylebook* or *The Chicago Guide to Style* can be referenced when you have questions about your writing style.

Chapter 11
Every Crisis Is an Opportunity

*"A lie can travel around the world
while the truth is putting on its shoes."*
—Mark Twain

S**t happens. A big part of public relations is crisis management, when you have to quickly control the potential damage a problem may cause or has caused. Although this is not our favorite part of the job, we've learned over the years that it's a hugely beneficial skill to have—not only in our work, but also in life. Knowing how to diffuse a bad situation with a combination of strategy and calm is an important tool for anyone to have in his or her coping arsenal. It's not just how you do in good times that shows what kind of person you are, but how you respond in bad times.

One of the best-known examples of crisis management done well was the Tylenol cyanide scare of 1982, after which Johnson & Johnson immediately recalled the product and halted all advertising, even though the company had nothing to do with its painkillers having been laced. Their quick action and preemptive response helped protect their reputation with consumers, and is now a case study in many business schools across the country. (Unfortunately, they didn't learn from their past; the company's 2010 product recall of everything from infant Tylenol to Benadryl was not dealt with quite as successfully.) Other more recent PR crises—all of which were handled poorly—include Toyota's recall of millions of faulty vehicles, presidential hopeful John Edwards's affair with Rielle Hunter, BP's oil spill in the Gulf of Mexico, and former British Prime Minister Gordon Brown being caught on tape calling a voter "bigoted" and his meeting with her "a disaster" (which contributed to Brown losing his re-election).

Crises happen to us all. Some are within our control and some are out of our control—but either way, your ability to handle them will determine whether you can rebound from a potential PR nightmare. In this chapter, we'll help you navigate through any crisis you may encounter in the workplace.

Key Message:
Put it in perspective

According to Maggie Gallant, senior vice president at Rogers & Cowan, "If you're dealing with a crisis, it's different now because of the 24-hour news cycle. It means you need to not panic and keep things in perspective.... When you're dealing with a crisis, it could seem like a big crisis to you, but not to others. If it's something with a coworker, sleep on it and deal with it the next day. Make sure that you're not making it a bigger deal than it is. Recognize that no mistake you or your client makes hasn't already happened to someone else. You can use everything that happens as an advantage. If you trip on your way into an office, laugh and use it as an icebreaker. The person interviewing you has tripped or has had a button pop off [too]."

Be a Problem-Solver

First and foremost, the best PR people are problem-solvers who demonstrate the ability to approach an emergency situation and quickly find a viable solution. Although people can often get overwhelmed or stymied when something goes wrong, it's exceedingly important to identify the issue, get the facts, and figure out the best way to handle the incident. Here are some tips on how to be a good problem-solver:

- **Find your zen zone.** Remember that your reaction sets the tone for the situation. Panic begets panic; anger incites more anger. We personally take a few deep breaths and sit quietly for a second before jumping back into the fray. With a clear focus, it's easier to search for a solution without anxiety or nerves getting in the way.

- **Use your noggin.** When faced with a tough predicament, rely on logic and creativity to come up with ways to approach the problem. In our business, a lot of PR folks rely on "no comment" as a response in a crisis; we believe there's always a better, more clever way to respond that doesn't sound like you're admitting guilt or trying to hide something. This may take a little extra brainpower and brainstorming, but it's worth exploring.

- **Consider the opportunity.** Rather than seeing a negative situation as a drag, try to view it as an opportunity to test your ability or to learn something. No obstacle is insurmountable. Observe how others have dealt with similar situations and whether you can learn from them. If you can successfully solve a problem, you'll be an asset to any company, client, or department.

 Sound Bite

"We can't learn to be creative until we accept the fact that we can fail. Every failure has a seed of lesson."
—Peter Shankman, founder of HARO

Hope for the Best, Prepare for the Worst

In public relations, when we see a red flag, no matter how early in the process, we try to either fix the problem before it happens, or at least prepare to face it when it does. For example, if we know that one of our clients is encountering business challenges or has a big personnel change on the horizon, we proactively come up with a strategy for how we'll respond if word gets out. Even if the potential crisis never sees the light of day, we know we have a statement ready in case it does. If you see a potential problem in the distance—whether it's a difficult client, a coworker who might sabotage a project of yours, or a deal that might fall through—think about how you would solve it or explain it before anything actually happens.

We refer to it as "getting ahead of the message," and it's a good practice.

Control the Damage, Clean up the Mess

So what if you are forced to face a crisis? Say, for example, that you stuck your foot in your mouth during an interview and accidently offended your interviewer, or you screwed up an assignment that your boss or client put you in charge of. You may think that there's no way to control the damage, but we say it's always worth a try. It's rare that a situation is entirely beyond repair. It may be very broken, but usually there's something salvageable. Take 2010's BP oil spill off the Louisiana shore, which we mentioned previously. There were a couple of big mistakes that were made early on, one being that the government took nine days to respond publicly and, two, that a viable solution wasn't reached fast enough. The most important step in solving that particular problem—which threatened our environment, as well as Louisiana's local fishing business—was to find a way to stop the losses, quite literally. Secondly, there should have been more open communication with the public—both by BP and the White House—about the situation and how it was being handled. Third, instead of playing a blame game, the oil industry and the U.S. government should have focused on cleaning up the mess. The numerous communications gaffes made along the way by BP Chairman Carl Henric-Svanberg and then CEO Tony Hayward certainly didn't help minimize the company's public relations disaster. And, in fact, they led to Hayward being forced to step down.

Now, you likely won't be faced with a crisis of that magnitude, but you can take some lessons from how those and others are handled and apply them to your own situation. For example, think about how you can address the damage quickly and effectively, using honest communication and problem-solving skills. Were you at fault, or did you contribute to the crisis in any way? Were there things you could have done differently to have avoided the situation? What can you do to fix the problem? How can you be honest and direct about the issue and its possible solutions? And how can you prepare next time so it doesn't happen again?

Own Up

Theodore Roosevelt once said, "In any moment of decision, the best thing you can do is the right thing, the next best thing is the wrong thing, and the worst thing you can do is nothing." If you make a mistake, admit it, learn from it, and don't do it again. When the U.S. soccer team lost to Ghana in the 2010 World Cup, midfielder Ricardo Clark, who allowed Ghana to score their opening goal, said, "I take full responsibility for letting my teammates down and I should have done better." When Facebook's privacy settings drew ire from consumers and press in May 2010, the company's CEO Mark Zuckerberg readily admitted that they'd "made a bunch of mistakes" and had "missed the mark." There's nothing worse than someone who refuses to take responsibility for his errors, lies about it, or blames others instead of owning up to what he did wrong. Case in point: When Senator (and vice presidential hopeful) John Edwards was accused of having an extramarital affair with a former campaign worker named Rielle Hunter in 2007, he publicly denied it, telling reporters, "The story is false. It's completely untrue, ridiculous." Two years later, Edwards finally admitted that not only had he had the affair, but he had also fathered Hunter's child. By not taking responsibility for his actions upfront, and then changing his tune so long after the initial crisis (not to mention cheating on his wife who, at the time, was battling cancer!), Edwards lost all credibility in the public's eye and ruined his political career.

Key Message:
Find the humor

Scott Cooke of GCK Partners transformed a possibly awkward moment into a long-term friendship and cover story: "I once set up a meeting for a fashion/stylist/retail client with a very important editor. My client was in his office, and the editor was running late. While hanging out in the boutique, I slipped off my cordovan wingtips and thoughtlessly started trying on high heels. Dressed in a suit and gabbing on the phone, I was walking around the shop in a size 12 pair of ultra-high Louboutin pumps and in walked the editor. She caught me mid-strut, and we've been best pals ever since. It was a very funny introduction to the brand and what my client does. The best news: It turned into a front page story—the client, that is—not me in the shoes."

Turn Trouble Into Triumph

You can't just throw up your hands and surrender when a crisis arises; too much is riding on the communication. Instead, try to stay positive and explore whether there's a way to turn lemons into lemon sorbet. Or, in our case, Irish stew. One of the magazines that Jessica oversees, *Good Housekeeping*, features a celebrity recipe in every issue. In honor of St. Patrick's Day, the magazine featured "Conan O'Brien's Irish Stew" in its March 2008 issue. As it turned out, the recipe wasn't his, which was discovered when Conan announced it on his show one night shortly after the magazine hit newsstands. He said that he had never made Irish stew, that he couldn't even make Ramen noodles, and he poked fun at the magazine for assuming that because he's Irish, he would be the celebrity to whom they attributed this traditional recipe. *Good Housekeeping*'s editors were absolutely mortified. Evidently, the service they used for celebrity recipes had made an error and it had not, in fact, been verified by Conan himself. The editor-in-chief was up in arms: *Good Housekeeping* and its research institute have a tremendous amount of credibility and consumer trust and, while innocent, this mistake posed a threat to that credibility.

But Jessica saw it differently. Why not lean into the wind and try to make it a positive PR opportunity? She suggested to her staff that they call the producers at *Late Night*, apologize for the error, and offer to make the Irish stew recipe for Conan so he could taste it on air. In addition, they invited him to come to the venerable Good Housekeeping Research Institute in midtown Manhattan and take a cooking class with the food director.

Well, his producers loved both ideas, and during the next week, what could have been a black mark on *Good Housekeeping*'s good name turned into a public relations bonanza—something money simply can't buy. First, Conan talked about how *Good Housekeeping* had apologized, and made some jokes about other celebrity recipes in the magazine. Then he appeared as a guest on Jay Leno's show and talked about the Irish stew incident. After that, the magazine's editor-in-chief went on *Late Night* and hand-delivered the Irish stew to Conan. Being a true comedian, Conan turned it into a hilarious skit—tasting the stew and then deciding it needed to be "more Irish," adding

Jameson's whiskey, Lucky Charms, and Irish Spring soap to the concoction. The editor presented him with a mock *Good Housekeeping* cover featuring his face and witty cover lines we had written just for the occasion.

But that wasn't all. About a week later, Conan came to the Good Housekeeping Research Institute to be a "guest tester." He and his crew filmed him taking a tour of the various labs, where he tested products and equipment, and interacted with the staff in comical ways. At the suggestion of the PR team, the magazine made him a personalized lab coat to wear during the segment (the sleeves of which were too short because he's 6'4"!).

The finished piece, which was funny, but also very informative about what goes on behind the scenes at the Good Housekeeping Research Institute, aired a few days later. We heard through the grapevine that *Good Housekeeping*'s competitors were envious that the magazine had gotten such amazing press, and wondered how on earth they had done it. It would have been easy to have issued an apology to Conan O'Brien, fire the celebrity recipe service (which was done anyway), and move on. But instead, Jessica and her team seized the opportunity to turn the situation in their favor. As former White House Chief of Staff Rahm Emanuel once said, "You never let a serious crisis go to waste...it's an opportunity to do things you think you could not do before." Now, he may have been referring to crises of world order, but the rule also applies to incorrectly attributed Irish stew!

We know that some of the best innovation comes out of challenges. Take Leigh Hurst, founder of the non-profit organization Feel Your Boobies, a foundation that utilizes innovative and unexpected methods to remind young women, primarily those under 40, to "feel their boobies."

Her personal story is one of overcoming obstacles. She founded the organization when she was diagnosed with breast cancer at the age of 33. What originally started with a few eye-catching t-shirts she designed to remind her friends to do self breast exams has evolved into a non-profit foundation and international campaign focused on spreading this life-saving message to young women using unexpected and unconventional methods.

So when she was faced with an overabundance of branded car magnets sitting in her basement, she set out to find a way to distribute them while spreading the word about the important cause. Her smart solution: She created the branded Boobies Bus, which she and a team used to travel around to speaking engagements and college appearances. The custom-wrapped, attention-grabbing vehicle—branded with pink polka dots, Feel Your Boobies logo, campaign graphics, and the slogan "Are you doing it?"—was a huge hit online, on college campuses, at events, and on the road. On the back of the bus was an invitation to "'Steal' a magnet. Spread the word." During that year, Feel Your Boobies gave away close to 5,000 magnets and traveled more than 15,000 miles to and from approximately 100 events. What started as a simple program evolved into a huge viral campaign, driving awareness and saving lives to boot.

Leigh shared, "As the person who primarily drives the bus, I have to say that it has definitely been wonderful to watch the reaction of those who come in contact with it. I've been privileged to overhear young girls in the grocery store parking lot ask their mother what the Boobies Bus means. Hearing the mother explain that it's about breast cancer and as you get older you need to feel your boobies for lumps simply gives me chills. Watching young college students get so excited to steal a magnet, or a young girl take a photo with her cell phone while passing the bus on the road, are things that inspire me to continue with this campaign. We've also received testimonials from women who believe the Feel Your Boobies Campaign is the reason they found their lumps and were diagnosed with breast cancer at an early stage. Several of these testimonials are from local women who have seen the bus."

Keep Things in Perspective

We have a saying in our business: it's PR, not the ER. When you're stressed out about a crisis, it may seem like the end of the world. Believe us, we're been there. But when that happens, take a moment to step back and put your situation in perspective. Things can always be worse: If you screwed up that interview and didn't get the job, there will be others. If you spilled your drink on someone at an important networking event, offer to pay their dry cleaning bill and move on.

Sound Bite

"There are no secrets to success. It is the result of preparation, hard work, and learning from failure."
—Colin Powell

So You Made a Mistake, but What Did You Learn?

Winston Churchill once said, "All men make mistakes, but only wise men learn from their mistakes." We're only human. We all slip up sometimes. Although it's never fun when mistakes happen, especially if they were easily avoidable, the important lesson to take away is whether you learned from the experience and how you can sidestep making the same error again in the future.

Years ago, one of the magazines Jessica worked with opened a celebrity showhouse in Los Angeles and wanted to do a press breakfast the day before to give previews to the local media. Not knowing the L.A. press all that well, but understanding that it was a totally different market from New York (where media folks can just hop on the subway for a walk-through), she felt it would likely be a waste, and cautioned the publisher against doing it. But he insisted, and so they proceeded. Only one person showed up and the event was a total bust, costing Jessica, her team, and the magazine's staff valuable time and money. Even though she had told the magazine that the breakfast was a bad idea, Jessica and her staff were blamed for its failure. But the experience served as a valuable reminder that *she*, not the publisher, was the PR expert and knew better than anyone else whether a press preview was worth doing. In hindsight, she should have put her foot down and demanded that the event be cancelled. Since then, she always asks herself and her clients whether an event is really necessary, or if their goals could be reached another way (in the case of the showhouse, for example, by sending a digital press kit and virtual house tour to the media before the opening).

News Flash:
Use the misstep
as a stepping stone

Linda Descano of Women & Co. was used to "hitting it out of the park" at work—until she shifted from running a corporate environmental risk program to working in portfolio management. "I learned quickly that I didn't have the desire or right mindset to be in portfolio management. While I loved interaction and clients, sales, pouring over balancing sheets, and selecting stocks was not me. It didn't ring true [and] felt like work. While it was hard to come to that realization, because I had invested a few years in becoming a CFA [certified financial analyst] charter holder, I had to step back to understand why and what I should do. I looked closely at the elements of the job that I like and what other positions I had held in the company–education, relationship, investment topics, clients, financial advisors—and began to explore opportunities. The misstep ultimately led to my position with Women & Co., and it offered me great lessons that I still utilize today."

Sound Bite

"Success seems to be
connected with action.
Successful people keep moving.
They make mistakes,
but they don't quit."
—Conrad Hilton

"Everyone Loves a Comeback"...
and Other Things to Learn From Other's Mistakes

1. **President Bill Clinton's affair with Monica Lewinsky.** Imagine being the most powerful man in the world, but not having the power to extricate yourself from a bad situation of your own doing. Today, however, Bill Clinton is seen as a strong, well-liked (by most) political figure who is the go-to guy for international negotiations. And, while still the punchline of many jokes, the crux of the Bill Clinton/Blue Dress scandal is that even the most public of missteps can be overcome with time, a lot of apologies, and focusing on others versus oneself.

2. **Martha Stewart's insider trading/prison term.** Though Martha Stewart's scandal unveiled cracks in her perfectly manicured image, her five-month sentence ended up doing more good than harm for her career. Having done her time, she was released from incarceration with a newly minted, more accessible air and attitude. Her (omni)media business has been steadily climbing ever since. The lesson: Do the crime, do the time, and then move on.

3. **Robert Downey Jr.'s "down and out" stretch.** From drug abuse to jail time, the gifted actor struggled in his personal life, negatively impacting his career. He was fired from films, and producers were loath to hire him because of the risk. He got help and, today, Downey has surpassed his previous success, thanks to top grossing films including Iron Man and Tropic Thunder.

The moral of his story is an old one: "It's always darkest before the dawn."

4. **David Letterman's affair with an employee.** Who could forget the day that David Letterman went on air with the news of his infidelity? Sure, having an affair was clearly the wrong thing to do, but the court of public opinion didn't judge Dave too harshly, thanks to some quick thinking and honest communication on his part. By owning up to what he did, his fans were able to move on.

Your Personal PR Action Plan

1. **Think of three examples of a "crisis" or misstep, and review how you handled them.** Did you remain calm? Were you able to come up with an alternative solution? If so, write up a case study for your use when challenges emerge. Take each incident and "rewrite" how you would handle it: Is there a way to infuse humor? Are there ways to salvage the scenario?

2. **Select one or two celebrity gaffes/crises that you've heard about.** Imagine if you were that person's publicist; how would you tackle the situation?

Conclusion

"If you want to be happy, set a goal that commands your thoughts,
liberates your energy, and inspires your hopes."
—Dale Carnegie

In the preceding pages, we talk about setting goals, mapping out a strategy, using creativity and confidence to stand out, making and leveraging connections—whether in the real or virtual world—and handling tough situations. But we'd be remiss not to revisit one of the 10 PR tenets that didn't get its own chapter, but is exceedingly important in one's career: Be passionate.

In most cases, people spend more time at work than elsewhere, so enjoying what you do every day is vital. When thinking about your career path, ask yourself: Does this job excite me? Does it allow me to flex my creative or strategic muscles? Will I look forward to coming to work each day? Do I find the people in this business/at this company engaging and easy to be around? Even if the job is challenging, will it also be fun, stimulating, and energizing?

The other part of cultivating that passion is having balance in your life. In PR, we typically operate "behind-the-scenes" while our clients get the spotlight, though we can often be in the line of fire when something goes awry. At the end of the day (especially a really tough day), we try to remind ourselves that no matter how hard we're working, we still have a life beyond the office that's just as important (if not more so) than our job. According to PR pro Heidi Krupp, "As publicists, we are absolute glorified caretakers. We like to make sure that our clients, our projects are handled with every detail…In business, you need to really define the boundaries for yourself and have a balance with your clients so you don't burn out." Or, as the old saying goes, "All work and no play makes Jack a dull boy."

This philosophy holds true, regardless of what industry you're in. It's important to take a step back, relax, and realize that whatever pressure you're under in the workplace is all relative. In these circumstances, think about what makes you happy—friends, your family, having a nice glass of wine, taking a yoga class, or playing basketball? Make sure you have other things in your life to focus on, particularly when your job (or lack thereof) is stressing you out. We all tend to get wrapped up in our work and lament when things don't go perfectly, but tomorrow is another day and harping on what went wrong won't help you move forward. Ultimately, being your own best publicist is about building a life—in and out of the workplace—that makes you happy and helps you shine.

We are lucky enough to love what we do. Sure, like anyone, we have days when we're frustrated, tired, and feel underappreciated, but overall, we find working in public relations to be challenging, creative, interesting and, yes, even fun. We hope that the advice we shared in this book also will help you have a fulfilling, engaging, and successful work life and to find your spot, centerstage.

 Sound Bite

"And in the end, the love you take is equal to the love you make."
—The Beatles

Recommended Reading

Black, Cathie. *Basic Black: The Essential Guide for Getting Ahead at Work (and in Life)*. New York: Crown Publishing/Random House, 2007.

Bloch, Phillip. *The Shopping Diet: Spend Less and Get More*. New York: Gallery Books/Simon & Schuster, 2010.

Bolles, Richard N. *What Color is Your Parachute? A Practical Manual for Job-Hunters and Career-Changers*. New York: Ten Speed Publishing/Random House, 2010.

Driver, Janine with Mariska van Aalst. *You Say More Than You Think: Use the New Body Language to Get What You Want!, The 7-day Plan*. New York: Crown Publishers/Random House, 2010.

Garcia, Nina with Ruben Toledo. *Nina Garcia's Look Book: What to Wear for Every Occasion*. New York: Hyperion/Harper Collins, 2010.

Lindstrom, Martin. *Buyology: Truth and Lies About Why We Buy*. New York: Broadway/Random House, 2008.

O'Conner, Patricia T. *Woe Is I: The Grammarphobe's Guide to Better English in Plain English, 3rd Edition*. New York: Riverhead Books/Penguin, 2009.

Pollak, Lindsey. *Getting from College to Career: 90 Things to Do Before You Join the Real World*. New York: Harper Collins, 2007.

Robinovitz, Karen and Melissa de la Cruz. *The Fashionista Files: Adventures in Four-Inch Heels and Faux Pas*. New York: Ballentine Books/Random House, 2004.

Schawbel, Dan. *Me 2.0: Build a Powerful Brand to Achieve Career Success*. New York: Kaplan Publishing, 2009.

Scott, David Meerman. *The New Rules of Marketing and PR: How to Use Social Media, Blogs, News Releases, On-line Video, and Viral Marketing to Reach Buyers Directly*. Hoboken, N.J.: John Wiley and Sons, Inc., 2007.

Shankman, Peter. *Can We Do That?! Outrageous PR Stunts That Work—And Why Your Company Needs Them*. Hoboken, N.J.: John Wiley and Sons, Inc., 2007.

———. *Customer Service: New Rules for a Social Media World*. Indiana: Que/Pearson Education, 2011.

Thebo, Kathy andJoyce Newman. *Selling Yourself: Be the Competent, Confident Person You Really Are!* New York: Mastermind Media, Ltd., 1994.

Touby, Laurel and Margit Feury Ragland. *Get a Freelance Life: mediabistro.com's Insider Guide to Freelance Writing*. New York: Three Rivers/ Random House, 2006.

Truss, Lynn. *Eats, Shoots & Leaves: The Zero Tolerance Approach to Punctuation*. New York: Gotham Books/ Penguin, 2003.

Wellington, Sheila and Betty Spence. *Be Your Own Mentor: Strategies from Top Women on the Secrets of Success*. New York: Random House, 2001.

Wood, Patti, MA, CSP. *Success Signals a Guide to Reading Body Language*. Oregon: Communications Dynamics, 2005.

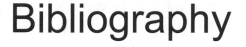

Bibliography

Introduction

"P.T. Barnum quotes." *Thinkexist*. October 2009. *http://thinkexist.com/quotes/P.T._Barnum*

"What Is PR?" *Chartered Institute of PR*. Chartered Institute of PR. UK. 1 August 2010 *www.cipr.co.uk/content/policy-resources/careers-pr/whatispr*.

Chapter 1

Black, Cathie. *Basic Black: The Essential Guide for Getting Ahead at Work (and in Life)*. New York: Crown Business/Random House, 2007.

Federer, Martin. "The Importance of Interpersonal Communication in a Family Business." *ezinearticles*. March 2010. *http://ezinearticles.com/?Importance-of-Interpersonal-Communication-in-a-Family-Business&id=2863471*

"Jim Rohn quotes." *Thinkexist.com*. May 2010. *http://thinkexist.com/quotation/effective_communication_is-what_you_know_and-how/295573*

Pincus, Aileen. "The Perfect (Elevator) Pitch." *Newsweek*. June 18, 2007. *http://www.businessweek.com/careers/ content/jun2007/ca20070618_134959.htm*

Chapter 2

"American proverb quotes." *Thinkexist.com*. March 2010. *http://en.thinkexist.com/quotes/american_proverb/2.html*

"The A-Team: Fun Stuff: Quotes." *imdb.com* June 2010. *http://www.imdb.com/title/tt0084967/quotes/*

"Benjamin Franklin quotes." *Thinkexist.com*. February 2010. *http://thinkexist.com/quotation/by_failing_to_prepare-you_are_preparing_to_fail/199949.html*

"Biography for Antoine de Saint-Exupery." *imdb.com* October 2009. *http://www.imdb.com/name/nm0756686/bio*

Booher, Diane. *The Voice of Authority: 10 Communications Strategies Every Leader Needs to Know*. New York: McGraw-Hill, 2007.

Khurana, Simran. "Lewis Carroll Quotes: *Alice in Wonderland*— Quotes From the Classic Novel *Alice in Wonderland*." *About. com Guide*. April 2010. *http://quotations.about.com/od/moretypes/a/alice4.htm*

Mazzeo, Tilar J. *The Widow Clicquot: The Story of A Champagne Empire and The Woman Who Rules It*. New York: Harper Collins, 2008.

Rizy, Christiaan, et al. *Business Meetings: The Case for Face to Face.* New York: Forbes Insights, 2009.

"10 PR stunts that would make PT Barnum proud." *PR Week.* December 22, 2009.

"Sun Tzu quotes" *Thinkexist.com* June 2010. *http://thinkexist. com/quotation/strategy_without_tactics_is_the_slowest_route_ to/220091.htm*

Chapter 3

"Benjamin Franklin quotes." *Brainyquotes.com.* June 2010.*www. brainyquote.com/quotes/quotes/b/benjaminfr141119.html*

"Bernard M. Baruch quotes." *Thinkexist.com.* June 2010. *http:// thinkexist.com/quotation/most_of_the_successful_people_i-ve_ known_are_the/147219.html*

"G.I. Joe: The Real American Hero." *Wikipedia.org.* June 2010. *http://en.wikipedia.org/wiki/G.I._Joe*

Chapter 4

Donne, John. "No Man Is An Island." *Poemhunter.com.* June 2010. *http://www.poemhunter.com/poem/no-man-is-an-island/*

"John F. Kennedy Inaugural Address." *Bartleby.com.* June 2010. *http://www.bartleby.com/124/pres56.html.*

Kile, Russell, et al. "Job Search Guide: Strategy for Professionals." *New York Department of Labor.* New York/Arlington. 3rd ed: 2006. *http://www.labor.state.ny.us/careerservices/findajob/ conduct.shtm*

"75% say Americans Getting Ruder." *Rasmussen Report.*September 22, 2009. *http://www.rasmussenreports.com/Public_content/ lifestyle/general_lifestyle/september_2009/75_say_americans_ are_getting_ruder.*

Chapter 5

"Arthur Ashe quotes." *FamousQuotesAbout.com*. May 2010. *http://www.famousquotesabout.com/by/Arthur-Ashe*

Gladwell, Malcom. *Blink: The Power of Thinking Without Thinking*. New York/Boston: Little, Brown & Co., 2005.

"Jerry Seinfeld quotes." *Thinkexist.com*. June 2010. *http://thinkexist.com/quotation/according_to_most_studies-people-s_number_one/9010.html*

"Quotations by Author: Alexander Graham Bell." *Quotations Page*. June 2010. *http://www.quotationspage.com/quotes/Alexander_Graham_Bell/*

Chapter 6

"Edward Gibbon quotes." *Brainyquote.com*. May 2010. *http://www.brainyquote.com/quotes/quotes/e/edwardgibb150889.html*

"Epictetus quotes" *Thinkexist.com* June 2010. *http://thinkexist.com/quotation/know-first-who_you_are-and_then_adorn_yourself/147581.html*

Hilton, Paris (with Merle Ginsberg). *Confessions of an Heiress: A Tongue-in-Chic Peek Behind the Pose*. New York:Fireside:, 2004.

Chapter 7

"Andy Warhol quotes." *Brainyquotes.com*. June 2010. *http://www.brainyquote.com/quotes/quotes/a/andywarhol109652.html*

"Oscar Wilde: Quotes." *The Free Library*. June 2010. *http://wildethefreelibrary.com/*

Wargo, Eric. "How Many Seconds to Make a First Impression?" *Association for Psychological Science*. July 2006. *http://www.psychologicalscience.org/observer/getArticle.cfm?id=2010*

Sample, Ian. "Ancient brain circuits light up so we can judge people on first impressions." *Guardian UK*. March 8, 2009. *http://www.guardian.co.uk/world/2009/mar/08/human-brain-circuit-impressions*

"Sylvester Stallone quotes." *Thinkexist.com*. May 2010. *http:/thinkexist.com/quotation/i_take_rejection_as_someone_blowing_a_bugle_in_my/220687.html*

Chapter 8

"Definition: Rainmaker." *Merriam-Webster*. June 2010. *http://www.merriam-webster.com/dictionary/rainmaker*

"Helen Nielsen quotes." *thinkexist.com*. June 2010. *http://thinkexist.com/quotation/humility_is_like_underwear-essential-but_indecent/197440.html*.

"Shakespeare quotes." *Absolute Shakespeare*. May 2010._*http://absoluteshakespeare.com/trivia/quotes/quotes.htm*.

Chapter 9

All, Sam. "Advisers all a-twitter over online networking? Hardly, IN survey reveals." *Investment News*. September 3, 2009. *http://www.investmentnews.com/apps/pbcs.dll/article?AID=/20090903/REG/909039981*

Du, We. "Job candidates getting tripped up by Facebook Job candidates getting tripped up by Facebook." *School Inc on MSNBC*. August 14, 2007. *http://www.msnbc.msn.com/id/20202935/*

Grove, Jennifer. "45% of Employers Now Screen Social Media Profiles." *Mashable*. August 19, 2009. *http:// mashable.com/2009/08/19/social-media-screening*

"Industry Facts." *Council of Public Relations Firms*. August 2010. *http://www.prquickstart.org/index.cfm?fuseaction=Page.viewPage&pageId=599&parentID=474*

"Kahlil Gibran quotes." *Quotations Page*. <wiki> June 2010. *http://www.quotationspage.com/quotes/Kahlil_Gibran/*

Slattery, Brennon. "Social Media Changes Old Web Habits." *PCWorld*. August 2, 2010. *http://www.pcworld.com/article/202357/ social_media_changes_old_web_habits.html*.

Chapter 10

"Emily Dickinson quotes." *Thinkexist* June 2010. *http:// en.thinkexist.com/quotes/emily_dickinson/*

"Estee Lauder (person): Quotes." *Wikipedia*. June 2010. *http:// en.wikipedia.org/wiki/Estée_Lauder_(person)*.

"Henry Beecher Ward quotes." *Thinkexist*. June 2010. *http:// thinkexist.com/quotation/ones_best_success_comes_after_their_ greatest/153247.html*

"James Dean: Personal quotes." *imdb*. June 2010. *http://www. imdb.com/name/nm0000015/bio*.

"Thomas Alva Edison quotes." *Thinkexist*. June 2010. *http:// thinkexist.com/quotation/opportunity_is_missed_by_most_people_because_it/12130.html*.

Chapter 11

"Colin Powell quotes." *Thinkexist*. June 2010. *http://thinkexist. com/quotation/there_are_no_secrets_to_success-it_is_the_ result/13079.html*.

"Conrad Hilton quotes." *Thinkexist*. June 2010. *http://thinkexist.com/ quotation/success_seems_to_be_connected_with_action/201932. html*.

"John Edwards denies affair with campaign worker." *LA Times*. October 13, 2007. *http://latimesblogs.latimes.com/washington/2007/10/breaking-news-j.html*.

Kirk, Jason. "Atlanta Native Ricardo Clark Struggles In World Cup Loss." *SBAtlanta*. June 27, 2010. *http://atlanta.sbnation. com/2010/6/27/1539720/atlanta-native-ricardo-clark*

"Mark Twain quotes." *Thinkexist*. June 2010. *http://thinkexist. com/quotation/a_lie_can_travel_halfway_around_the_world_ while/189781.html*

"Winston Churchill quotes." *Thinkexist*. June 2010. *http:// thinkexist.com/quotation/all_men_make_mistakes-but_only_ wise_men_learn/15788.html.*

Conclusion

Dale Carnegie Quotes and Quotations." *Famous Quotes and Authors*. September 2010. *http://www.famousquotesandauthors. com/authors/dale_carnegie_quotes.html*

Lennon, John and McCartney, Paul. "The End (song lyrics)." *Wikipedia*. September 2010. *http://en.wikipedia.org/wiki/The_ End_(The_Beatles_song)*

Index

About the
Authors

Jessica Kleiman is vice president of public relations for Hearst Magazines, one of the world's largest publishers of monthly magazines, where she oversees all public relations efforts for the magazine division of Hearst Corporation, including 14 consumer titles in the U.S., such as *Cosmopolitan*, *Esquire*, and *O, The Oprah Magazine*; digital media; international; brand development; and integrated media. She has worked both in-house and on the agency side for the past 15 years.

Kleiman has guest lectured about magazine publicity at both New York University and the Columbia Publishing Course at Columbia University. She has also written articles for publications including the *New York Post*, *The Resident* (a free New York city weekly), *Seventeen*, and *Weight Watchers Magazine*. She lives in Brooklyn, New York, with her husband and daughter. Kleiman keeps her love for the English language alive on her blog, *Funny Word of the Day*.

Meryl Weinsaft Cooper joined DeVries Public Relations as managing director of the Home & Lifestyle division in Fall 2010, following her tenure as senior vice president/partner at LaForce + Stevens. While at L+S, she led programs for a variety of hospitality, spirits, and consumer clients, and was the driving force behind the company's mentoring and philanthropy programs.

Her 15-plus years of PR experience include stints in art, music, and entertainment, including time at the Screen Actors Guild's New York office. She lives in Brooklyn, New York, with her husband and dog, and spends her spare time writing and producing films, and seeking out the best culinary, travel, and art experiences, which she documents in her blog, *Searching for Jake Ryan*.